A Two-Tiered Theory of Control

Linguistic Inquiry Monographs
Samuel Jay Keyser, general editor

A complete list of books published in the Linguistic Inquiry Monographs series appears at the back of this book.

A Two-Tiered Theory of Control

Idan Landau

The MIT Press
Cambridge, Massachusetts
London, England

This book was set in Times Roman by Toppan Best-set Premedia Limited, Hong Kong.

Library of Congress Cataloging-in-Publication Data

Landau, Idan.
A two-tiered theory of control / Idan Landau.
  pages cm. – (Linguistic inquiry monographs)
Includes bibliographical references and index.
ISBN 978-0-262-02885-1 (hardcover : alk. paper) – ISBN
978-0-262-52736-1 (pbk. : alk. paper)
1. Control (Linguistics) 2. Grammar, Comparative and general–Verb phrases.
3. Grammar, Comparative and general–Sentence particles. I. Title.
P299.C596L38 2015
415–dc23

                                                    2014042765

Contents

Series Foreword

We are pleased to present the seventy-first volume in the series *Linguistic Inquiry Monographs*. These monographs present new and original research beyond the scope of the article. We hope they will benefit our field by bringing to it perspectives that will stimulate further research and insight.

Originally published in limited edition, the *Linguistic Inquiry Monographs* are now more widely available. This change is due to the great interest engendered by the series and by the needs of a growing readership. The editors thank the readers for their support and welcome suggestions about future directions for the series.

Samuel Jay Keyser
for the Editorial Board

Preface

Sometimes one hits upon a new theory thanks to a fortuitous combination of circumstances.

In the spring of 2011, I was invited to take part in the celebration of the 50th anniversary of MIT's graduate program in linguistics, to be held in December that year. This scientific reunion spanned from the earliest generation of linguists educated at MIT, to the most recent. Accordingly, the organizers instructed the speakers to present their topic of interest within a historical perspective. It so happened that during that time I was completing a survey book on my own topic of interest, the theory of control (Landau 2013), and indeed, the opening sections of that book outlined a short intellectual history of control in generative grammar. The invitation sounded like an excellent opportunity to present this work to an audience that would probably include some of the key figures who helped shape that history.

As I was looking for a narrative "spine" for my presentation, the theme of the "duality of obligatory control" suggested itself almost immediately. This theme, in different guises and within different frameworks, runs through so many studies of control that it must hold some fundamental truth—so I assumed. At that point, I was only interested in hunting down the duality theme and detecting intellectual connections between seemingly disparate theoretical schools or approaches to the topic of control. Developing a *new* theory was certainly not on my agenda after completing such a comprehensive survey of facts and theories of control.

Still, I felt that the historical narrative should lead to current-day work, and that this work should somehow reinterpret the duality theme, perhaps even throw new light on it. So the end of my presentation—the last two pages of the handout—sketched some ideas about predication and logophoricity that could be fruitfully applied in the domain of obligatory control.

These sketchy, impressionistic, noncommittal, hand-waved ideas turned out to be the start of the two-tiered theory of control, which this book is all about.

They nearly made their way to the dustbin, but for some reason they stubbornly clung to my desktop. I leave it to the reader to judge whether this was a stroke of luck or not.

In retrospect, I can trace quite a few points of discontent with available work on control, including my own earlier work, that lay behind my decision to embark on this project. Possibly the deepest one was the realization that for four decades, two research traditions on control, rich with analysis and insight, have proceeded in parallel, yet in nearly total disconnect: one in formal semantics, the other in generative syntax. This disconnect was not only harmful to the study of control but also out of synch with current linguistic theory, which places an ever-growing emphasis on the syntax-semantics interface.

As I began trying to bridge this gap, it became clear how wide it is. Fundamental assumptions in the formal semantic treatments of control and in the syntactic treatments were mutually incompatible. For example: Prevalent explanations of the *de se* reading of PRO in obligatory control could not explain the basic fact that PRO displays grammatical agreement with the controller. Conversely, prevalent syntactic explanations of the agreement fact could not come to terms with the *de se* semantics. Another issue was the over-reliance on parochial, theory-internal devices in deriving the crosslinguistic distribution of control complements.

These and other concerns motivated my attempt to take a fresh look at some of the classical problems. The result is ambitious enough to be called a "theory," but at the same time it leaves quite a few open ends that will hopefully inspire further research.

Finally, I would like to acknowledge my intellectual debt to people who have generously shared their time and thoughts with me as this book was taking shape: Valentina Bianchi, Thomas Grano, Peter Herbeck, Orin Percus, Philippe Schlenker, and two anonymous reviewers for MIT Press. I have had the fortune to present the essentials of this work in linguistics colloquia at the University of Chicago, Tel Aviv University, the Hebrew University of Jerusalem, and the University of Athens. Without doubt, the feedback I received from all these individuals and audiences has saved this study from some serious errors of fact and judgment.

I dedicate this book to all those who spend years and decades working on the same topic and never stop marveling at the most elementary puzzles that lured them in the first place.

1 Introduction

There is a curious schism in the generative scholarship of control, going back to the early 1970s, between the work done in syntax and typology and the work done in formal semantics. While a great deal has been discovered about the nature of control within these two research strands, very few attempts have been made to compare and correlate their results within a broader theory that encompasses all the major facets of control. An attempt to formulate such a theory is presented in this book. At the same time, the theory to be developed revives and reinterprets a persistent intuition running through much of the classical work: that the unitary appearance of obligatory control (OC) into complements conceals an underlying *duality* of structure and mechanism.

Concretely, I will propose that OC is established either through *predicative* control or through *logophoric* control. Empirically, the former applies in non-attitude complements, the latter in attitude complements. In predicative control, the complement is a property-denoting projection, while in logophoric control, it is a propositional projection constructed as a second tier above the predicative complement—hence the term *two-tiered theory of control* (TTC). Furthermore, while predicative complements establish OC via simple predication, logophoric complements establish OC via variable binding, the bound variable being a projected coordinate of the embedded context of evaluation. Crucially, in both types the element known as PRO functions as a property-creating abstractor.

In this analysis, the characteristic *de se* reading in logophoric control arises as a special case of *de re* ascription, induced by the OC complementizer, and *not* by local operator binding or indexical shift, the more common devices in previous studies. The argument rests on the premise that only this analysis involves direct variable binding by the controller, and variable binding in OC plays a key role in explaining a fundamental asymmetry in the crosslinguistic distribution of predicative vs. logophoric complements. Thus, I present a striking case of syntactic typology *choosing* among semantically equivalent analyses (of obligatory *de se* in OC). I also show that other syntactic and semantic properties differentiate the two types of control, bolstering the two-tiered theory on independent grounds.

As already mentioned, the duality of OC is an old idea, and it is useful to set the stage by taking a quick look at the considerations that lay behind it.[1] The first generative study of control, Rosenbaum 1967, already distinguished between complements where the nonfinite VP is only dominated by S (VP complements) and those where it is dominated by NP/PP over S (NP/PP complements); the distinction had to do with the absence or presence of "nominal" behavior under passive or pseudocleft formation.[2] Interestingly, Rosenbaum focused on formulating the Equi-NP Deletion rule (which deleted the controllee under coreference with the controller), skirting the fundamental question of *why* coreference is obligatory in some cases and merely optional in others.

This latter question became the key criterion for later studies that highlighted the dual nature of OC. Focusing on English, the question was how to distinguish between structures where an OC complement alternates with a *for*-infinitive with a lexical subject and structures where OC is the only option.

(1) a. Bill$_i$ agreed PRO$_{i/*j}$/for Mary to join the club.   *OC or for-NP*
    b. Bill$_i$ condescended PRO$_{i/*j}$/*for Mary to join the club.   *Only OC*

For Chomsky and Lasnik (1977), "control" in structures of type (1a) involved the deletion of a reflexive pronoun (Refl-Deletion, or in short, Equi) whereas structures of type (1b) involved obligatory control of PRO, a wholly distinct derivation. The distinction itself, however, was encoded as a lexical feature and was left unexplained.

Williams (1980) took the same empirical cut to reveal the contrast between optional coindexing and predication. For Williams, optional coindexing was a species of nonobligatory control (NOC), so that cases like (1a) were put in the same basket as cases like *John$_i$ agreed that [PRO$_{i/j}$/Mary$_j$ joining the club] would be a step forward*. This was a terminological pitfall, as PRO in the former is clearly under the obligatory control of *John*, unlike PRO in the latter, a genuine case of NOC. Nevertheless, the idea that one type of OC (though not necessarily coextensive with what Williams had in mind) reduces to syntactic predication was enormously influential and indeed is adopted in this book as well.

Parallel work in other theories the 1980s continued to reformulate the duality of OC on the same, uncontested empirical grounds. Work in Lexical-Functional Grammar (LFG) identified Williams's OC with *functional* control (structure sharing at f-structure) and his NOC with *anaphoric* control (coindexing with a functional anaphor—namely, PRO); see Bresnan 1982, Mohanan 1983. Work in Government-Binding (GB) Theory hypothesized that PRO is pronominal in CP complements (type (1a)) and anaphoric in IP complements (type (1b)); see Bouchard 1984, Koster 1984.

Perhaps the gravest problem with this line of research was its primary focus on English and its highly exceptional (in typological terms) *for*-infinitive construction. In fact, even within English the availability of this construction is subject to a great deal of variation. The sole criterion of allowing/disallowing a lexical subject proves to be a poor predictor of other systematic properties of OC complements.[3] Without abandoning the insight that OC splits into two types, later studies aimed at placing the distinction on a firmer, typologically informed empirical ground. Thus, Wurmbrand (2003) and Grano (2012) capitalize on the distinction between restructuring and nonrestructuring complements (equivalently for Wurmbrand, property-denoting VPs vs. propositional TP/CP complements). In Landau 2000, 2004, 2006b, I model control on the basic operation Agree, which may apply through two "routes": directly to PRO or indirectly via C, depending on whether the complement does or does not bear semantic tense. Each route is associated with its own syntactic and semantic properties.

The starting point of the present study is my Agree model, and in particular, a crosslinguistic generalization stated in Landau 2004. In essence, I will distill the empirical content of that work while discarding most of its theoretical apparatus. Restating these findings in terms of the predicative/logophoric distinction mentioned above will make it possible to explore a fundamentally different approach to the duality of OC. In so doing, I will follow insights of Williams (1992) and Bianchi (2003). Williams posited the very same distinction in the realm of adjunct control, arguing that adjuncts exhibit a split between direct predication and logophoric antecedence. Bianchi assimilated control into attitude complements to logophoric dependencies, remaining neutral on the type of control operative in nonattitude complements.[4]

The structure of this book is as follows. Chapter 2 lays out the Agree model: the fundamental assumptions, the distinction between tensed and untensed complements, the distinction between partial and exhaustive control, the typological predictions, and the formal apparatus. The chapter ends by listing seven fundamental problems with this model that motivate a different approach.

Chapter 3 then develops the proposal: the TTC. It shows that the Agree model's tense distinction can (and probably should) be restated in terms of attitude/nonattitude complements, proposes and defends the notion that PRO is a minimal pronoun, and analyzes predicative control in terms of PRO-movement-as-abstraction. It then turns to logophoric control, considering and ultimately rejecting two semantic approaches to the problem of obligatory *de se*: indexical shift and local operator binding. An alternative in terms of a special *de re* presupposition is presented, whose major advantage is the natural explanation it affords for the agreement aspects of control and, in particular, the crosslinguistic generalization discussed in chapter 2.

Chapter 4 broadens the empirical purview of the TTC by looking at three further distinctions that surprisingly align with the two types of control: logophoric but not predicative control requires a [+human] PRO; logophoric but not predicative control allows an implicit controller; and logophoric but not predicative control allows control shift. All three distinctions straightforwardly follow from basic properties of the TTC.

Chapter 5 offers preliminary thoughts on still further interactions with partial and split control, controlled lexical pronouns/reflexives, and noncanonical topic control (in Philippine languages). Although the chapter does not offer full-blown analyses of these phenomena, it shows that they pose no substantial challenge to the TTC, and it suggests some plausible extensions to accommodate them.

Finally, chapter 6 takes a broader look at how the results of this book shed light on control into adjuncts and NOC, raising the intriguing possibility of a higher-level unification of all control constructions under a single roof.

2 The Agree Model: Fundamentals

The Agree model of OC has been developed and expanded over a decade in a series of works.[1] In this chapter, I discuss the conceptual basis of the model as well as the core empirical motivation behind it. In section 2.1, I discuss the typological coverage of the model and its application to different complement types in different languages. In section 2.2, I present the formal apparatus of the model and the interaction of [T]/[Agr] features with the Agree relations that establish OC. In section 2.3, I raise several concerns, mostly theoretical but also empirical, that call for substantial revisions in the model.

Before I lay out the model, some definitions are in order.[2] First, I distinguish between OC complements and *no-control* (NC) complements. The former host an anaphor-like null subject, OC PRO, with the familiar properties (locally controlled, sloppy reading under ellipsis, etc.). The latter host a lexical DP or a null pronoun (*pro*) subject, which are exempt from control. This distinction is *different* from the standard distinction between OC and nonobligatory control (NOC), although the two are occasionally (and regrettably) confused. NOC clauses typically occupy subject and adjunct positions, not complement positions, and they host a PRO subject, not a DP/ *pro* subject, the former falling under logophoric interpretation. I barely touch on NOC in this book (though see chapter 6 for some comments); in fact, it is far from clear that complement clauses ever display NOC (see Landau 2013:43–46 for discussion of this point). The choice is always between OC and NC.[3]

Second, I define a complement clause as *tensed* if its temporal coordinate need not coincide with that of the matrix clause. The definition is semantic and independent of morphological tense (e.g., there are tensed infinitive clauses and there are untensed subjunctive clauses). It also cuts across the gerund/infinitive divide, pace Stowell 1982. I recognize two types of tensed complements: realis ones (subsuming propositional and factive complements) and irrealis ones (subsuming desiderative and interrogative complements). The test for the [±T] value of a clause consists in the (im)possibility of introducing conflicting temporal modifiers in the matrix and the embedded clauses, as illustrated in (2).

(2) a. *Yesterday, John condescended to join us   *implicative-[−T]*
       tomorrow.
    b. Yesterday, John agreed to join us tomorrow.   *desiderative-[+T]*
    c. *Yesterday, Mary remembered to call us   *implicative-[−T]*
       last week.
    d. Yesterday, Mary remembered calling us last   *factive-[+T]*
       week.

The phenomenon of *partial control (PC)* is keyed to the [±T] distinction (Landau 2000; see also Wurmbrand 2003, Grano 2012, Pearson 2013, Landau to appear). Nonfinite *tensed* complements allow their null subject to be construed as a group properly including the controller (together with some contextually salient participants); *untensed* complements impose strict identity between them (*exhaustive control (EC)*).

(3) a. *James$_i$ condescended [PRO$_{i+}$ to meet] thanks to our pressures.
    b. James$_i$ agreed [PRO$_{i+}$ to meet] thanks to our pressures.

Finally, I define a complement as *inflected* or as [+Agr] if it carries visible inflection for φ-features (either on Aux or on the main predicate). This criterion sets infinitives and gerunds apart from indicative/subjunctive clauses, as well as from inflected infinitives.[4]

The [±T] criterion breaks down control complements into two categories, each consisting of four subclasses. Sample members of these categories are given in (4) and (5).[5]

(4) *Predicates selecting untensed complements [−T]*
    a. *Implicative*
       avoid, bother, compel, condescend, dare, decline, fail, force, forget, get, make sure, manage, neglect, refrain, remember, see fit
    b. *Aspectual*
       begin, continue, finish, resume, start, stop
    c. *Modal*
       have, is able, may, must, need, should
    d. *Evaluative (adjectives)*
       bold, cowardly, crazy, cruel, (im)polite, kind, modest, rude, silly, smart

(5) *Predicates selecting tensed complements [+T]*
   a. *Factive*
      dislike, glad, hate, like, loathe, regret, sad, shocked, sorry, surprised
   b. *Propositional*
      affirm, assert, believe, claim, declare, deny, imagine, pretend, say, suppose, think
   c. *Desiderative*
      afraid, agree, arrange, aspire, choose, decide, demand, eager, hope, intend, mean, offer, plan, prefer, promise, ready, refuse, resolve, strive, want, yearn
   d. *Interrogative*
      ask, contemplate, deliberate, find out, grasp, guess, inquire, interrogate, know, unclear, understand, wonder

These predicates merge with different types of complements, in different languages, to yield OC or NC. The complements may differ in category (IP vs. CP vs. DP), mood (indicative vs. subjunctive), or morphological tense (subjunctive vs. infinitive), but each one falls on a definite side of the [±Agr] divide. The other grammatical features do not matter. The fundamental claim of the Agree model is that *all we need to know* about the control behavior of a complement (whether it displays OC or NC) are two pieces of information: the value of its [T] feature and the value of its [Agr] feature.

The overarching generalization is this:

(6) *The OC-NC generalization*
   In a fully specified complement clause (i.e., a clause in which the I head carries slots for both [T] and [Agr]):
   a. If the I head carries both semantic tense and agreement ([+T,+Agr]), NC obtains.
   b. Elsewhere, OC obtains.

The generalization is restricted to "nondefective" complement clauses—namely, standard infinitives (whose I head bears [−Agr], "abstract agreement"), subjunctive complements, and indicative complements. Excluded are raising/ECM (exceptional case-marking) complements and small clauses, where either [T] or [Agr] (or both) are entirely missing (see Landau 2004), and subject/adjunct clauses.

(6) is an elsewhere rule. The fundamental insight behind it is simple: OC is the elsewhere case of NC. In other words, the natural class is the set of clauses where lexical DPs and *pro* are licensed as subjects. PRO is licensed in a heterogeneous class of environments—in particular, whenever the I head

is specified [+T,–Agr], [–T,+Agr], or [–T,–Agr]. (6) is currently the only successful description of the crosslinguistic patterning of OC and NC complements.[6]

2.1 Typological Predictions

Consider the typological predictions of this theory. Fully specified clauses ([+T,+Agr]) fall under NC. These are standard indicative clauses, as well as subjunctive clauses in many languages (e.g., Romance and Slavic), which indeed never display OC.[7]

OC complements will be found in two contexts, as follows.

(7) *Typological predictions: OC complements*
   a. Untensed complements (excluding small clauses) will universally be in the OC class, *regardless of inflection.* More concretely, the predicates in (4) will form the universal core of control verbs.
   b. Uninflected complements (i.e., [–Agr]) that are nevertheless nondefective (so a [T] slot is present) will universally be in the OC class, *regardless of semantic tense.*

The predictions are confirmed across a wide range of languages and constructions, as shown in Landau 2004, 2006, 2013. What follows are sample illustrations.

Consider first (7a). Unsurprisingly, untensed and uninflected infinitives (in English and other languages) induce OC (8a). Less trivially, untensed but inflected complements still induce OC. This possibility is manifested either in controlled subjunctives in the Balkan languages ((8b), from Varlokosta 1993) or in controlled inflected infinitives in Hungarian ((8c), from Tóth 2000).

(8) a. *OC in [–T,–Agr] infinitives: English*
      Mary$_i$ remembered/forgot [PRO$_{i/*j}$/*Bill to lock the door].
   b. *OC in [–T,+Agr] subjunctives: Greek*
      O   Yanis   kseri   na   kolimbai   (*o   Giorgos).
      the   John.NOM   knows   prt   swim.3SG   (*the   George.NOM)
      'John knows how (*George) to swim.'
   c. *OC in [–T,+Agr] inflected infinitives: Hungarian*
      Kellemetlen   volt   Péternek$_i$ [PRO$_i$/*pro$_j$/*neki$_{i/j}$/*Katinak
      unpleasant   was   Peter.DAT   PRO/*pro/him.DAT/*Kate.DAT
      későn   érkez-ni-e].
      late   arrive-INF-3SG
      'It was unpleasant for Peter [PRO$_{i/*j}$/*for him/*for Kate to arrive late].'

Moving to (7b), uninflected complements always induce OC. This was already shown for untensed infinitives (8a), and it holds equally for tensed infinitives (9a). Less trivially, OC is induced in such complements even in languages that exhibit inflected infinitives elsewhere, like Welsh (see (9b), from Tallerman 1998); note that lexical pronouns fuse with the infinitival marker in this language.

(9) a. *OC in [+T,−Agr] infinitives: English*
Mary$_i$ planned/hated [PRO$_{i/*j}$/*Bill to lock the door].

b. *OC in [+T,−Agr] uninflected infinitives: Welsh*

Gwnaeth	Elen	gytuno	[i/*iddi	ddarllen	y	llyfr].
did	Elen	agree	to/*to.3FEM.SG	read	the	book

'Elen agreed to read the book.'

Turning now to NC complements, the prediction from (6) is as follows:

(10) *Typological predictions: NC complements*
Complements that are tensed and inflected will be uncontrolled, *regardless of mood.*

I have already mentioned that this is the typical situation with indicative complements. Observe now that the NC character cuts across the different moods, solely depending on the presence of [+T,+Agr].[8] Tensed subjunctives in Balkan languages display NC; compare (11a) with (8b). Tensed inflected infinitives in European Portuguese display NC; compare (11b) with (8c) (Hungarian has no direct counterparts). And tensed inflected infinitives in Welsh also display NC; compare (11c) with (9b). ((11a–c) are from Varlokosta 1993, Raposo 1987, and Tallerman 1998, respectively.)

(11) a. *NC in [+T,+Agr] subjunctives: Greek*

O	Yanis	elpizi	na	figi	(o	Giorgos).
the	John.NOM	hopes	prt	leave.3SG	(the	George.NOM)

'John hopes to leave.'/'John hopes that George would leave.'

b. *NC in [+T,+Agr] inflected infinitives: European Portuguese*

Eu penso/afirmo	[ter-em	os deputados	trabalhado	pouco].
I think/claim	to.have-3PL	the deputies	worked	little

'I think that the deputies have worked a little bit.'

c. *NC in [+T,+Agr] inflected infinitives: Welsh*

Disgwyliodd	Aled	[iddi	hi/*pro*	fynd].
expected	Aled	to.3FEM.SG	she/*pro*	go

'Aled expected her to go.'

A vivid illustration of the role of agreement comes from cases where the *same* predicate selects either a [+T,−Agr] or a [+T,+Agr] complement, the

mood remaining constant. Such pairs are found in languages with a suffi-
ciently rich complementation system, like Turkish. In this language, both
OC and NC are realized in nominalized clauses. The nominalizing suffix
-*mE* (glossed in (12) as INF) takes either inflected or uninflected clauses,
agreement being reflected by possessive markers. A predicate like *korkmak*
'afraid', which selects irrealis tense on its complement, will induce NC or
OC depending on whether the complement is inflected or not (Słodowicz
2007).

(12) a. *OC in [+T,–Agr] nominalized complements: Turkish*
    Ahmet$_i$ [PRO$_{i/*j}$ düş-mek]-ten   kork-uyor-du.
    Ahmet PRO   fall-INF-ABL   fear-PROG-PST.3SG
    'Ahmet was afraid to fall.'
  b. *NC in [+T,+Agr] nominalized complements: Turkish*
    Ahmet$_i$ [*pro*$_{?i/j}$ düş-me-sin]-den   kork-uyor-du.
    Ahmet pro   fall-INF-3SG-ABL   fear-PROG-PST.3SG
    'Ahmet was afraid that he would fall.'

To summarize, a very broad and diversified array of crosslinguistic data
supports the idea behind (6): namely, NC is guaranteed by the cooccurrence
of semantic tense and morphological agreement on the inflectional head in the
complement, and OC obtains elsewhere. This is the empirical content of the
original Agree model, and as we just saw, it can be stated and substantiated in
relatively theory-neutral terms.[9] In fact, this empirical content will be carried
over in toto to the new, "dual theory" to be developed in chapter 3. First,
however, I will describe the formal characteristics of the Agree model and then
present the problems that call for its revision.

2.2 The Formal Apparatus of the Agree Model

Consider first Tense selection. If the complement is bigger than TP, selection
must be indirect, given that the semantic tense operator is located in the
complement T, which is separated from the matrix predicate (at least) by a CP
projection. We assume, then, that the matrix predicate selects an uninterpretable T ([uT]) value on C, which in turn must be checked against a matching
interpretable T ([iT]) value on the lower T.

(13) *The syntax of selected tense*

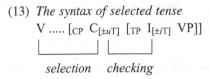

    selection   checking

The basic analytic challenge is to establish a systematic link between the "clausal features," [T] and [Agr], and the referential features of the complement subject. Following a traditional approach, PRO is marked as [−R(eferential)] and DP/*pro* as [+R(eferential)]. These are interpretable features; in the Agree model, they have uninterpretable counterparts on T and C. The uninterpretable feature, [uR], is automatically generated on [T,Agr] bundles according to the following redundancy rule:

(14) [R]-*Assignment Rule*
     For $X_{[\alpha T, \beta Agr]} \in$ {I, C, ...}:
     a. $\varnothing \rightarrow$ [+uR] / $X_{[\_\_]}$, if $\alpha = \beta =$ '+'
     b. $\varnothing \rightarrow$ [−uR] / elsewhere

Thus, the following types of I heads emerge: [+T,+Agr,+uR], [+T,−Agr,−uR], [−T,+Agr,−uR], and [−T,−Agr,−uR] (again, ignoring "defective" and reduced clauses).

Being uninterpretable, [uR] probes for a matching feature on a local goal, using standard clause-internal Agree. The closest nominal element that is c-commanded by the complement T is the complement subject (in its vP-internal base position). To match [+uR], that subject must be [+iR]—namely, a lexical DP/*pro*. To match [−uR], that subject must be [−iR]—namely, PRO. A lexical DP/*pro* subject occurring with $T_{[−uR]}$ or a PRO subject occurring with $T_{[+uR]}$ would leave the [uR] feature on T unchecked, causing the derivation to crash. The OC-NC generalization in (6) is thus captured.[10]

The more innovative part of the model also attributes the OC effect itself to Agree. Specifically, a matrix functional head forms an Agree relation with a φ-bearing element in the infinitive—either an Agr bundle or PRO. The matrix functional head, functioning as the probe, is the same head that enters an Agree relation with the controller DP—T for subject control, light v for object control, or some applicative head for oblique controllers. [Agr] is accessible as a goal only on the C head of the infinitive, given that the next lower Agr bundle is on T, which is lower than PRO, a potential goal itself. Thus, there are two control routes: one is direct to PRO, the other is mediated by C.[11]

(15) *PRO–control*
     ... T/v ... DP ... [CP C [TP PRO[φ] T]]

(16) *C–control*
     ...T/v ... DP ... [CP C[φ] [TP PRO[φ] T]]

Three assumptions underlie this picture. First, a "tensed" C (i.e., specified [+T]) may be selected with or without [Agr] (depending on the language, on the matrix predicate, etc.); untensed C (specified [−T]) lacks [Agr] altogether. If [Agr] is selected, the C control route is taken, since C is closer to T/v than PRO. If C is Agr-less, PRO control is the only option.

Second, the infinitival CP is not a strong phase in Chomsky's (2001) sense. It cannot be one since by definition, a strong phase is a syntactic substructure inside which all the features have been valued. Yet the φ-features of PRO are not valued until the requisite Agree relation is formed with a matrix element. The implication is that OC complements—assuming they are CPs—are weak phases.

Third, in order to transmit the necessary φ-values, the matrix T/v must be first valued by the controller DP; T/v then enters two Agree relations. The controller DP (in its base position) does not induce intervention for the second Agree relation precisely because it is the goal of the first Agree relation. This circumvention of the Minimal Link Condition is licensed by the Principle of Minimal Compliance (Richards 1998), an instance of Multiple Agree (Hiraiwa 2005).

The distinction between PRO control and C control is relevant to the explanation of partial control; it also interacts with case transmission in Russian in an intriguing way (Landau 2008). For now, we may abstract away from this distinction and return to the traditional description of control as a relation between a matrix DP and PRO.

2.3   Unsatisfactory Aspects of the Agree Model

For all its success in deriving the OC-NC generalization, the Agree model cannot be the final word on control, for it raises at least seven independent problems. The problems are not unique to this specific model; most are shared with many other models. Nevertheless, any attempt to improve on this model must first recognize its limitations. I discuss them briefly below.

1. *The Stipulative [R]-Assignment Rule.* Although the specification of the features [T] and [Agr] is independently motivated, as is the distinction between DP/*pro* and PRO in terms of their [R] value, the system retains an arbitrary kernel. First, [R] is taken as a primitive feature, begging the question of what underlying morphosyntactic properties determine its value. Second, and more importantly, there is no inherent logic to the association of [+T,+Agr] with [+R] and the complementary association of other [T]-[Agr] combinations with [−R], other than a faint formal resemblance. This is no small matter. In fact, it is the heart of the matter: only by virtue of the associations in (14) can the

OC-NC generalization be captured. Furthermore, the uninterpretable variant, [*u*R], has no distinct morphological expression (nor is there any morphological reflex of its polarity), raising the suspicion that it is no more than a theory-internal convenience.

True, the Agree model is on equal footing with virtually all alternative theories of control on this fundamental point. None of them offers any insightful answer to the question, "Why do certain complement types force a PRO subject and others a DP/*pro* subject?"[12] As mentioned above, previous accounts were no less stipulative (invoking unmotivated assumptions about government, or factually incorrect assumptions about Case). Yet there is little solace in this equality; perhaps we can do better.

2. *Triggering.* The model appeals to the formal operation Agree, yet it is not clear what triggers the operation in OC configurations. It cannot be the matrix functional head, for all the uninterpretable features of that head are already checked against the DP controller by the time the complement clause is probed. What about the possibility of a low trigger? In PRO–control (15), the only candidate is the [−*i*R] feature on PRO. Although interpretable, this feature is anaphoric, and presumably Agree with a valued antecedent "satisfies" it. The intuition is clear, but whether Agree is capable of delivering such semantic outcomes is less clear. In C–control (16), however, there is not even a candidate for a low trigger; the [−*u*R] on C can be checked against [−*i*R] on PRO (and the same for [−Agr]). Not being interpretable itself, [−*u*R] is not an anaphor. This still leaves the anaphoric [−*i*R] on PRO without a valued antecedent; but again, it falls short of providing direct triggering (Agree (T$_{Matrix}$,C) would have to be "altruistic" for the benefit of PRO).[13]

3. *The Coherence of "Semantic Tense".* Recent work suggests that the notion of "semantic tense" is more nuanced than assumed in the Agree model. On the basis of sequence-of-tense diagnostics, Wurmbrand (2014) distinguishes among simultaneous (aspectual and implicative) infinitives, which project up to Asp(ect)P, modal (irrealis) infinitives, and "zero-tense" (propositional) infinitives; none of them, according to Wurmbrand, contain contentful tense, although they give rise to different temporal interpretations. Following up on Wurmbrand's results, Grano (2012) points out "oddballs" for the Agree model: EC predicates that allow temporal mismatch (thanks to modality) and PC predicates that do not. These developments suggest either that the PC class is linguistically spurious, or that it is indeed real but what makes it stick together is not tense but some other linguistic concept.

4. *The Status of PRO.* It is no secret that PRO is a sore thumb in the eyes of many linguists. The problem is not so much its nullness (although certain frameworks, such as Categorial Grammar, are already averse to this property)

as its uniqueness to control environments. Attempts to reduce PRO to more fundamental elements go back to the GB era and form a cornerstone of the present-day movement theory of control (Hornstein 1999, Boeckx and Hornstein 2006, Boeckx, Hornstein, and Nunes 2010). The most popular ideas are to view PRO either as an anaphor or as a copy (trace) of movement. In contrast, the Agree model did not concern itself with eliminating PRO but simply suggested that it is an anaphoric element "of sorts" (akin to SE anaphors). Moreover, the reduction of PRO to trace raises numerous empirical difficulties.[14]

The question remains—why is PRO confined to control environments? Any theory that takes PRO to be a nominal element that can, in principle, occur elsewhere is to be preferred on grounds of conceptual simplicity (assuming the theory passes the hurdle of empirical adequacy, a prerequisite for this kind of consideration).

5. *The (lack of) Relation between OC and NOC.* Early generative treatments of control upheld a uniform structural constraint on both OC and NOC (Grinder 1970), but this position was soon discarded on empirical grounds (see Landau 2013 for a historical overview). Two alternatives emerged: (i) PRO in NOC is a pronoun; (ii) PRO in NOC is a logophor. Crucially, on either approach, OC PRO is an unrelated category (anaphor, trace, variable, etc.). The Agree model adopts the logophoric analysis of NOC, which proves to be superior to the pronominal analysis. Yet it too falls short of bridging the gap between the identity of OC PRO and the identity of NOC PRO. Correlatively, the mechanisms involved in assigning reference to the two elements are sharply distinguished (OC being determined jointly by the lexicon and syntax, NOC being a discourse phenomenon). While the empirical differences are undeniable, it is legitimate to ask whether they run as deep as an ontological duality of PRO rather than reflecting higher-level grammatical distinctions that nonetheless hide a unitary structure.

6. *Semantic Groundedness.* The Agree model is chiefly concerned with agreement and feature transmission, but says very little about the interpretation of OC constructions. Once again, this is not a problem specific to the Agree model, yet it is one that should ultimately be addressed in a comprehensive theory of control. In Landau 2000, I propose that Agree establishes coindexing, which in turn is interpreted as variable binding (more precisely, the controlling and the controlled thematic positions are variables co-bound by the same operator). It would be good to see a more explicit account of the syntax-semantics interface in OC constructions, which would also address the less canonical situations of partial and split control.

7. *Oblique Control.* When the controller is a prepositional object (e.g., *We demanded from him to turn himself in, Can I impose upon you to share this information with us?*), the matrix probe is the applicative head that licenses the controller. This assumption is problematic in two respects. First, PPs are presumably precisely the kind of arguments that are *not* introduced by applicative heads; the latter are called upon to integrate bare DP arguments (Baker 1988, Marantz 1993). Second, even if such an applicative head exists, it is unlikely to register the ϕ-features of the prepositional object. Such objects typically do not control agreement; when they do, the agreement shows up on the preposition that governs them (Baker 2008) and not on any functional head in the verbal projection. But in the absence of a functional head that registers the ϕ-features of the controller DP, there is no probe for the Agree operation that establishes OC. This is a serious problem, for oblique control is a very common option in many languages.

After developing the new analysis of control, I return to these issues in section 3.8.

3 A New Proposal: Predication vs. Logophoric Anchoring

This chapter develops a comprehensive theory of OC that supersedes the Agree model. Discarding much of the technical apparatus of that model, the new theory retains its major two achievements: first, the dichotomy between EC and PC complements, and second, the OC-NC generalization. Both of these achievements will have to be restated so as to make them amenable to a rather different treatment of control, one that pays closer attention to semantic considerations.

In section 3.1, I recast the EC/PC distinction in terms of the underlying semantic notion of attitude reports: PC verbs are attitudinal, while EC verbs are not. In section 3.2, I propose that PRO is treated as a minimal pronoun in *all* of its manifestations. In section 3.3, I present the analysis of EC complements as a type of predication, made possible by the movement of PRO, which abstracts over the complement. In section 3.4, I address PC complements: after discussing the shortcomings of two alternative accounts (indexical shift and local binding of a logophor), I propose that logophoric control is constructed as a second tier above the structure produced for predicate control; the link to the matrix clause is established by a bound variable denoting a coordinate of the embedded context and projected as an argument of the complementizer, which also introduces the special *de se* presupposition. How the two modes of control support agreement between the controller and PRO is addressed in section 3.5, where the notion of Feature Transmission at PF is explicitly developed. This forms the basis of section 3.6, where the OC-NC generalization is fully derived. In section 3.7, I contrast the mechanism of Feature Transmission at PF with the mechanism of Feature Deletion at LF, arguing that the latter is confined to nonlocal variable binding. Finally, in section 3.8 I return to the problems noted earlier regarding the Agree model and show how they are solved within the new system.

3.1   Attitude and Nonattitude Contexts: Restating the Split

So far, we have seen that the two types of OC complements differ in two respects. One type is semantically untensed and rejects partial control (EC complements); the other type is semantically tensed and allows partial control (PC complements). These two properties are correlated in Landau 2000 via certain assumptions about the way [T] and [Agr] bundle in control complements. Importantly, the underlying intuition there is that the two properties are not ontologically symmetric, one being a theoretical primitive, the other a derivative. It is the contrast in [±T] that explains the contrast in (the partiality of) control, and not vice versa. What I would like to propose now is a shift in perspective, whereby *both* properties stem from a third, still deeper distinction: whether the complement is selected by an attitude predicate or not.[1]

Attitude contexts are domains in which the denotation of linguistic expressions is determined relative to the epistemic or bouletic state of a participant in the reported situation and not relative to the actual world. Insofar as specific descriptions may mean different things for different people (i.e., pick out different referents in their respective belief worlds), referential expressions are known to give rise to the *de re/de dicto* ambiguity. Thus, the presence of such an ambiguity is a standard test for attitude contexts (and its absence, for nonattitude contexts).[2]

Because it is ambiguous between the two readings, a definite description cannot be substituted *salva veritate* inside an attitude context, the way it can inside a nonattitude context. Suppose Ralph, an old acquaintance of Bill, has been appointed the new boss in Bill's office, but Bill does not know this yet. The following contrast in entailment patterns indicates that the complement of *see* is not an attitude context whereas that of *imagine* is:

(17)   a.   Bill saw Ralph jogging in the park.
        ⇒   Bill saw the new boss jogging in the park.
       b.   Bill imagined Ralph jogging in the park.
        ⇏   Bill imagined the new boss jogging in the park.

In this light, consider EC and PC control verbs. It is easy to see that modal, aspectual, and evaluative predicates select nonattitude complements, whereas desiderative, propositional, and interrogative predicates select attitude complements. The examples in (18) and (19) are representative of each subclass; they should be evaluated in the context introduced above.

(18)   *EC complements: Nonattitude contexts*
        a.   Bill should greet Ralph.   *modal*
         ⇒   Bill should greet the new boss.

    b.   Bill started to talk to Ralph.   *aspectual*
    ⇒   Bill started to talk to the new boss.
    c.   It was rude of Bill to ignore Ralph.   *evaluative*
    ⇒   It was rude of Bill to ignore the new boss.

(19) *PC complements: Attitude contexts*
    a.   Bill planned to meet Ralph soon.   *desiderative*
    ⇏   Bill planned to meet the new boss soon.
    b.   Bill pretended to be Ralph.   *propositional*
    ⇏   Bill pretended to be the new boss.
    c.   Bill asked where to take Ralph for lunch.   *interrogative*
    ⇏   Bill asked where to take the new boss for lunch.

It is slightly less obvious that implicative verbs (especially those involving an Experiencer subject) select nonattitude complements.[3] To see that this is indeed the case, contrast implicative with factive verbs, which take attitude complements. The contradiction test is equivalent to the entailment test but is somewhat easier to judge.

(20) a. Bill remembered to greet Ralph,   *implicative*
         # but he didn't remember to greet the new boss.
    b. Bill remembered greeting Ralph,   *factive*
         but he didn't remember greeting the new boss.

Suppose the second conjunct of (20a) were true. If Bill didn't remember to greet the new boss, it follows that he didn't greet the new boss, which entails, in turn, that he didn't greet Ralph. But if he didn't greet Ralph, then the first conjunct of (20a) would be false, contrary to the assertion. The second conjunct of (20b), on the other hand, does not entail that Bill didn't greet the new boss (in fact, it retains the entailment that he did). Not knowing who Ralph was, Bill may have no memory of greeting *the new boss*, so the two conjuncts are consistent.[4]

    As Pearson (2013:406) observes, implicative complements are not semantically opaque, and so indefinite DPs inside them carry existence entailments, unlike their behavior inside attitude complements.

(21) a. #John dared/remembered/saw fit to ride a unicorn.
    b. John wanted/refused/agreed to ride a unicorn.

The basic split in the OC domain can now be restated as follows:

(22) Nonattitude complements are untensed and force EC;
      attitude complements are tensed and allow PC.

One can see why the two types of complements might differ in their temporal properties. Attitude domains are evaluated relative to alternative (nonactual) contexts, and one coordinate of such contexts is the time coordinate; thus, John's belief worlds may be situated in the past (if he is thinking of past events) and his bouletic worlds are situated in the future (in which his desires will be fulfilled). So the presence of semantic tense is a by-product of attitude contexts; put in grammatical terms, [+T] is introduced by attitude operators.

Reference to semantic tense in infinitives may be misguided, however, in view of recent evidence that they exhibit no semantic tense (Wurmbrand 2014); rather, irrealis infinitives contain a modal operator and other infinitives are either tenseless or contain a "zero tense." If this is true, the present discussion allows us to discard all reference to tense in describing control complements, by simply focusing on the attitude property.[5]

(23) Nonattitude complements force EC; attitude complements allow PC.

This feature of the new theory improves over the original Agree model. In that model, the [±T] distinction was a stipulated selectional distinction imposed by the matrix verb. This is not to say that it was arbitrary; being a semantic property, it was couched in the lexical semantics of different control verbs. Nevertheless, the distinction was *unrelated* to any other semantic aspect of control verbs, thus missing the robust correlations in (23). Viewing the tense contrast as a manifestation of the deeper contrast in (non)attitude contexts removes this anomaly. Furthermore, we will shortly see that the attitude operator introduced by PC verbs carries more information beyond (a possibly null) tense—specifically, logophoric coordinates encoding the speech event participants—that constitutes the control dependency. Thus, there is little doubt that the shift in perspective is a step forward in understanding the mechanisms of control.

The attitude/nonattitude distinction allows a restatement not only of the EC/PC contrast, but also of the OC/NC contrast—that is, the very generalization regulating the distribution of OC complements. The OC-NC generalization in (6) states that the cooccurrence of semantic tense and agreement on a complement's head blocks control. Since semantic tense is now replaced by an attitude context, and the latter induces logophoric control, we can restate the generalization as a contrastive effect of inflection on the two types of control. Again, direct reference to tense is unnecessary.

(24) *The OC-NC generalization (restated)*
    [+Agr] blocks control in attitude complements but not in nonattitude complements.
    Or:
    [+Agr] blocks logophoric control but not predicative control.

Equivalently, a complement clause whose head is inflected for ϕ-features may display either predicative control or no control at all, but may not display logophoric control. Explaining this curious interaction is the task of section 3.5.

I will now lay out the formal analysis of the two types of control, starting with what they share: the element PRO.

3.2 PRO as a Bound Minimal Pronoun

Predicative and logophoric control complements display very distinct properties. I have already mentioned that predicative complements are nonattitude contexts that impose EC, while logophoric complements are attitude contexts that allow PC. Further contrasts, to be discussed below, include *de se/de re* readings, tolerance for implicit control, and control shift. One may ask whether the distinction goes down to the level of the controlled element. That is, are there two types of OC PRO, one occurring in predicative complements, the other in logophoric ones, each associated with its own characteristic interpretation?

This question is not far-fetched, and in fact, the semantic literature develops various proposals along these lines. The idea is that in attitude OC complements, PRO is bound by a logophoric or context-shifting operator, lexically encoded in the attitude predicate or syntactically present as an operator in the C–domain of the complement. This binding relation generates the obligatory *de se* interpretation. To guarantee the binding relation, PRO is "flagged" by a diacritic: [+author] in Schlenker 2003 (reflecting the 1st person perspective of *de se*), [log] in Anand 2006 (matching the logophoric operator), [log] in Maier 2011 (triggering an acquaintance presupposition of identity to the attitude holder), both [log] and [loc] in von Stechow 2003 (the latter encoding the necessary locality of the operator to PRO), and [J] in Stephenson 2010 (referring to the perspectival "center").

There are four problems with this family of proposals. First, as Anand (2006:63) admits, they are openly stipulative, reifying basic structural and interpretive aspects of OC as lexical markers instead of deriving them from deeper principles. Second, they raise several empirical as well as theoretical difficulties (see sections 3.4.2–3.4.3). Third, there is no causal connection whatsoever between the form of PRO and its featural content. Why is it overwhelmingly the case that a bound variable with any of these diacritics ends up being phonetically null?[6] On some proposals, PRO is featurally identical to logophoric pronouns, which are of course overt. The difference is in their licensing environments, but again, it is not clear what is it about the environments that makes PRO null and logophoric pronouns overt. These are the kinds of questions that an integrated theory of control must address.

The final problem with the semantic proposals is that they cannot extend to instances of PRO in nonattitude contexts, where no logophoric (or context-shifting) binder is present in C. As Chierchia (1990) observed early on, any attempt to pin the *de se* reading of OC PRO down to some inherent feature it bears would falsely predict that all instances of OC PRO should support this reading.[7] In fact, quite a few OC contexts are free of the *de se* entailment. These are precisely the contexts of predicative control, unmediated by a log-ophoric operator. Note that the controller need not be human, and even when it is, it bears no 1st person epistemic relation to the embedded event (see also Safir 2010, from which examples (25a–b) and (26a,c–d) are drawn, Sundaresan 2010, Landau 2013, and Pearson 2013:541).

(25) a. This key$_i$ will serve/do [PRO$_i$ to open the door].
 b. The accident$_i$ is responsible [for PRO$_i$ causing the ship to sink].
 c. The apartment$_i$ failed [PRO$_i$ to meet the federal housing quality standards].
 d. The transmission problem forced the car$_i$ [PRO$_i$ to stop].

(26) a. Mavis screamed at/mumbled to Toby$_i$ [PRO$_i$ to batten the hatches] (but he never heard her).
 b. The master of ceremonies signaled to the amnesiac$_i$ [PRO$_i$ to leave the stage].
 c. John$_i$ managed [PRO$_i$ to avoid the draft] (because he spent that decade in a coma).
 d. Mary$_i$ neglected [PRO$_i$ to send the payment].

Other instances of nonlogophoric PRO involve infinitival main predicates, subject relatives, and subject purpose clauses.

(27) a. [This cheesecake]$_i$ is [PRO$_i$ to cheer you up].
 b. I wait to hear the song$_i$ [PRO$_i$ to be selected].
 c. I bought this blender$_i$ [PRO$_i$ to help me make split pea soup].

In the face of examples like those in (25)–(27), the semantic proposals mentioned above would be forced to posit a second kind of PRO, basically a simple λ-abstracted variable. Thus, they are committed to a dual analysis: PRO$_{[author/log/loc]}$ in attitude contexts, and a simple PRO elsewhere. This seems like a suspicious duplication of the grammatical information already present in the two types of contexts PRO occurs in: attitude and nonattitude contexts. A preferable solution would posit a *single* element PRO, unspecified for any particular interpretation. Specific meanings would arise from the grammatical contexts rather than from any inherent feature on PRO.

This leads to a radically impoverished view of PRO: a "reference variable" in the sense of Sigurðsson 2008 or a "minimal pronoun" in the sense of Kratzer 2009. I will adopt this view in what follows. For concreteness, assume the following lexical entry ([$u\phi$] stands for unvalued ϕ-features):

(28) *A minimal pronoun*
     X is a minimal pronoun if and only if X = [D,$u\phi$].

Within different derivations, X can become a reflexive, a bound lexical pronoun, a resumptive pronoun, a *pro* element identified by local agreement, a relative pronoun, or indeed, controlled PRO. The choice among these options is determined by a combination of the syntactic context and the lexical inventory of the language.[8]

For example, a relative pronoun will be formed when the C head of the relative clause assigns the feature [+wh] to the minimal pronoun (assuming, of course, that the language has relative pronouns). Reflexives, if available, will preempt pronouns in local binding configurations (Condition A contexts). This can be guaranteed either by endowing the binder with a [+refl] feature (Kratzer 2009) or by formally distinguishing local from nonlocal dependencies (syntactic Agree vs. semantic variable binding), as in Reuland 2010, 2011. The actual reflection of the transmitted features on the bound element will depend on the morphological specificity of the item, as well as on language-particular rules of Spell-Out resolution. Quite often, simplex reflexives are not specified for number or gender (e.g., French *se*, Dutch *zich*); in the absence of a "recipient slot," these features will not be reflected on the bindee, vocabulary insertion being conditioned by the familiar Subset Principle. Thus, minimal pronouns may well vary in the range and specificity of their morphological makeup. What is common to all of them is the obligatory inheritance of ϕ-values from the binder *for whatever feature slots they are specified for.* I return to these observations in section 3.5 and formalize them in (69).

Within this general context, PRO is but one realization of the generalized grammatical element, a minimal pronoun. This view eliminates the "specialness" of PRO, a sore thumb for most earlier accounts (see point 4 in section 2.3). I take it that any account that multiplies the lexical entry of PRO beyond this single, minimal element bears a rather heavy burden of proof. This consideration will be very effective in narrowing down the available analytic options in what follows.

As for the distinction between predicative and logophoric control, the minimal pronoun approach places the explanatory burden on the detailed specification of the syntactic and semantic ways in which these two environments are distinguished. I now provide a formal analysis of the two cases, starting with predicative control.

3.3 Predicative Control: PRO Movement

Predicative control is found with four classes of predicates (see (4)): aspectual, modal, implicative, and evaluative. As discussed in section 3.1, the complements of these predicates are nonattitude contexts.

(29) a. Mary began to paint the wall.
   b. Mary is able to paint the wall.
   c. Mary saw fit to paint the wall.
   d. It was smart of Mary to paint the wall.

Note that the embedded event is entailed only in (29c–d); in (29a), only the beginning of the process of painting is entailed, while in (29b), there is reference to a potentiality (the embedded event holds in all of the possible worlds in which Mary's abilities are materialized). The nonattitude property reflects the fact that the evaluation of the embedded event does not depend on the epistemic or bouletic state of the controller, Mary; rather, it depends on physical or external conditions.[9]

As an example, let us consider the verb *begin*, using the semantics of the progressive aspect as a model (Condoravdi 2009); for a comparable treatment of implicative verbs, see Pearson 2013:410–413. If John began to paint the wall in world w, then John has painted the wall to some degree d (lower than 1) in w; further, it is reasonably expected that in some world w′ where things develop in ways most compatible with the past course of events in w, called an *inertia world* of w, John paints the wall to a greater degree.

(30) *Definitions*
   a. $IN_w =_{def} \{w': w'$ is an inertia world of $w\}$
   b. $e \subset e'$ if and only if e is an initial subevent of e'.

The denotations of the predicative complement and the control verb are given in (31).

(31) a. $[\![\text{to paint the wall}]\!]^{w,g} = \lambda d'.\lambda x.\lambda e'.e'$ is an event of x painting the wall to degree d' in w
   b. $[\![\text{begin}]\!]^{w,g} = \lambda P_{<d,<e,<s,t>>>}.\lambda d'.\lambda x.\lambda e'.P(d',x,e') = 1$ in w $\wedge$ Cause (x,e') in w $\wedge \exists <e'',w'',d''> [w'' \in IN_w \wedge e' \subset e'' \wedge d' < d''], P(d'',x,e'') = 1$ in w″
   c. $[\![\text{begin to paint the wall}]\!]^{w,g} = \lambda d'.\lambda x.\lambda e'.e'$ is an event of x painting the wall to degree d' in w and x causes e' in w and $\exists <e'',w'',d''> [w'' \in IN_w \wedge e' \subset e'' \wedge d' < d''], e''$ is an event of x painting the wall to degree d'' in w″.

Importantly, the predicative relation between *Mary* and *to paint the wall* is established syntactically and is visible to both LF and PF. In other words, in predicative control, the relation between the complement and the controller is registered at all grammatical levels and not just in the semantics. This of course echoes the line of research originating in Williams 1980, where predication was conceived as a core syntactic relation. I follow this intuition with one important departure: in the present analysis, syntactic predication accounts only for one subtype of OC (in fact, the less frequent one); logophoric control utilizes a different device (see section 3.4).

Let us now consider the syntax of predicative control. The two key components in any predication relation are a referential argument and a predicate. In predicative control, the former is the controller and the latter is the infinitive.[10] The two stand in a mutual m-command relation, which is standardly taken to be the relevant locality condition on syntactic predication.

If the complement to the control verb is a lexical projection, predication is straightforward, since lexical projections can function as natural predicates. Such is the case in radical restructuring, where the infinitive hosts no structural subject and projects to the VP level only (Wurmbrand 2003). I set aside this option, which does not seem to raise any particular difficulty.

More interesting are situations where the infinitive is headed by some functional category (Asp, T, Fin, etc.). These categories project phrases that are not natural predicates, and become predicative only with the aid of a syntactic operator. Thus, a clause is turned into a predicate by an operator merged at its edge, either externally or internally (by movement); the operator is later translated as a λ-abstractor. This device is put to use in relative clauses, *tough*-constructions, object purpose clauses, parasitic gap constructions, left dislocation, and copy-raising constructions (see Landau 2011 for discussion).

Is the operator in predicative control merged externally or by movement? The two options are semantically equivalent, but there may be syntactic reasons to favor one over the other. Below, I will mention some reasons for preferring the movement option. Under this analysis, the operator is nothing but PRO itself, moving to the specifier position of the infinitival complementizer. This is, of course, not a new idea. It was Chomsky (1980) who first proposed PRO movement as a means of producing syntactic predication in infinitival purpose clauses. Hendrick (1988) recruited PRO movement for relative clause formation in general, and Clark (1990) extended it to all OC constructions. My implementation follows Clark's insights, but restricts them to predicative control only.[11]

The derivation of predicative control proceeds as follows. An infinitival TP with a PRO subject is embedded under a "predicative" head in the low

CP periphery. I will designate this head as *Fin* (Rizzi 1997), reserving the label *C* for the head of logophoric control complements; nothing crucial rests on these labels, however. Like the C head of a relative clause, Fin attracts an operator to its specifier. Unlike the former, though, the latter requires a nominal operator (i.e., a D category); call this Fin head a *transitive Fin*. Let us encode this property by an uninterpretable feature on Fin, [*u*D], that acts as a probe searching for a matching D category. The closest one is of course PRO, in Spec,TP, which is therefore pulled up and remerged in Spec,FinP. The predicative FinP is subsequently merged as the complement of the lexical control verb, in the case of subject control, or the complement of a causative small clause, in the case of object control. I illustrate the former first, showing the derivation of *John managed to stay healthy* in (32).

(32) *Derivation of predicative subject control*

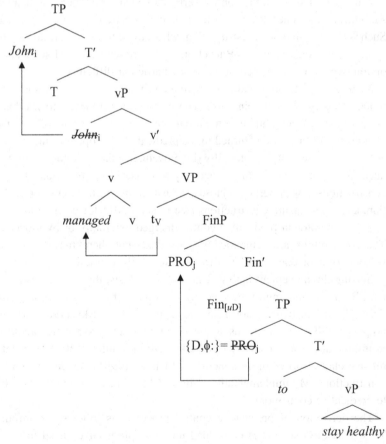

A few comments are in order about this derivation. As defined in (28), the embedded subject is nothing but a minimal pronoun; I retain the symbol *PRO* for expository convenience only. Also suppressed are higher projections in the CP periphery, which could serve as landing sites for focus or *wh*-elements. Just as infinitival complements of *tough*-constructions are not rendered islands by the occurrence of a null operator at their edge (e.g., *Where are red pebbles most difficult to find?*), standard control complements are not either.

A major benefit of this analysis is that it automatically delivers the fundamental distributional property of control: the subjecthood of PRO. The controlled nominal is the one that is attracted to Spec,Fin and creates the λ-abstract. Since this movement is triggered by feature checking (to satisfy [uD] on Fin), which is subject to the Minimal Link Condition, the attracted nominal must be the closest one to Fin, namely, the subject. Thus, the subjecthood of PRO is derived with no recourse to unmotivated stipulations concerning case or government (see McFadden 2005 and Landau 2006b for discussion).

Furthermore, placing the triggering feature on the Fin head (selected by the control verb) rather than on PRO immediately explains why PRO's movement is maximally local. Compare, in this regard, the related proposal by Pearson (2013:536), where PRO is also treated as a (minimal) abstractor that undergoes Ā-movement to the edge of its clause. Differently from the present proposal, Pearson's stipulates that PRO is inherently specified as a pronoun that "must move." Putting aside implementation—exactly what syntactic feature has that consequence?—this wrongly permits long-distance movement of PRO (just like that of relative pronouns), overgenerating examples like **Mary_i said [PRO_i that John claimed [t_i [t_i to be true to herself]]]*. As far as I can tell, even the necessary subjecthood of PRO is not derived on this analysis.

Another noteworthy feature of the structure in (32) is that the predicative relation is an emergent property and not encoded in any specific ingredient. Thus, unlike in related proposals in the literature, there is neither a [+pred] feature nor a designated "operator" in (32). λ-abstraction is an automatic outcome of movement (Heim and Kratzer 1998). The fact that the moved element (PRO) does not saturate the λ-predicate formed thereby follows naturally from its being merely a nonreferential numerical index. In other words, the radical impoverishment of a minimal pronoun allows it to turn into an operator, once moved. The trace of PRO, equally devoid of content, serves as the variable abstracted over. From the standpoint of LF, PRO is nothing but a numerical index, interpreted as an operator in Spec,FinP and a variable in Spec,TP, the difference being purely configurational (contingent on movement) and not inherent. Precisely in virtue of lacking any intrinsic content,

PRO in predicative control imposes no semantic restrictions on its antecedent (25), just as PRO in other predicative environments does not (27).

In (32), the complement comes to denote the predicate $\lambda x.x$ *stay healthy*. This predicate is truly nonpropositional, lacking any temporal specification (see (4)). Thanks to V-to-v raising in the matrix clause, the m-command domain of the complement is the matrix vP. Syntactic predication is thus licensed, with v serving as the *relator* in Den Dikken's (2006) sense. In the semantics, the open property denoted by the FinP projection is applied to the referent of *John*, obtaining the saturated state of affairs *stay-healthy(John)*. The implicative verb, of course, makes its own contribution to the overall interpretation, similarly to the aspectual verb in (31b) (see Pearson 2013:410–413).

Another basic property of OC complements—the ban on lexical subjects— is derived too. Suppose a lexical DP is merged as the internal subject of the embedded vP and raised through Spec,TP to Spec,FinP, as in (33a). Then FinP comes to denote a proposition (type $\langle s,t \rangle$), in violation of the lexical requirement of the control verb, which selects a property (type $\langle e,\langle s,t \rangle \rangle$, abstracting away from the degree argument) as an internal argument (cf. (31b)).[12] The same is true if both a lexical DP and PRO are merged in the complement clause and PRO only moves as high as Spec,TP, (33b). If it is the DP that moves and PRO stays, (33c–d), the structure is presumably uninterpretable, since vP denotes a proposition, which cannot combine with the nominal in Spec,Fin via predication. In addition, (33c–d) incur a violation of the θ-Criterion, as the DP and PRO compete over a single θ-role.

(33) a. $*[_{FinP}$ DP$_i$ Fin $[_{TP}$ t$_i$ T $[_{vP}$ t$_i$ v $[_{VP}$ ...]]]]
    b. $*[_{FinP}$ DP Fin $[_{TP}$ PRO$_i$ T $[_{vP}$ t$_i$ v $[_{VP}$ ...]]]]
    c. $*[_{FinP}$ PRO Fin $[_{TP}$ DP$_i$ T $[_{vP}$ t$_i$ v $[_{VP}$ ...]]]]
    d. $*[_{FinP}$ DP$_i$ Fin $[_{TP}$ t$_i$ T $[_{vP}$ PRO v $[_{VP}$ ...]]]]

The question remains why PRO cannot be replaced by a lexical pronoun; in traditional terms, what explains the nullness of PRO? In fact, this property is common but not universal. In chapter 5, I return to discuss the privileged status of null forms as the choice for minimal pronouns, in both predicative and logophoric control.

The structure of predicate object control is slightly more complex. Observe that the rather small class that participates in this construction consists of implicative verbs only, all of which are semantically causative (e.g., *force*, *compel*, *coerce*, *impose*). Assume, then, that the object controller and the infinitive occupy the subject and predicate positions of a small clause, projected by a predicative head, or a relator; RP is the maximal projection of this relator, serving as the complement of the causative verb.[13] (33) illustrates the derivation of *John forced Bill to stay home*.

(34) *Derivation of predicative object control*

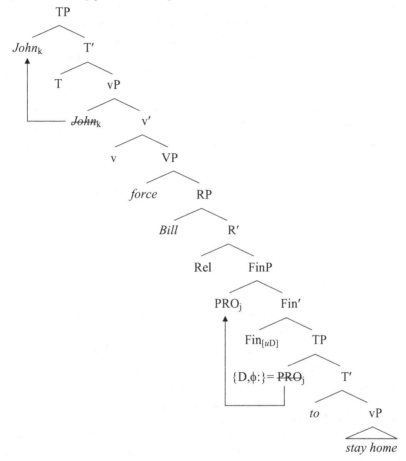

On the PF side, syntactic predication is a vehicle of agreement; all φ-features of the subject are copied onto the predicate. The details of this process are elaborated in section 3.5. Because syntactic predication is a highly rigid relation, predicative control exhibits a number of restrictions of which the other type of control—the logophoric type—is free. (I return to these contrasts in chapter 4). Surprisingly, predicative control is less restricted in one empirical domain: interaction with inflection. As stated in (24), predicative control holds regardless of inflection, whereas logophoric control is contingent on the absence of [+Agr]. The reason for this independence of syntactic predication and inflection will become clear in section 3.6.

Finally, let me point out one side benefit of the particular view I take on transitive-predicative complementizers. The feature on Fin responsible for attracting the PRO operator, I suggested, is [uD]. Note that this feature characterizes another syntactic category: prepositions. The category P is defined by the very same selectional property: it selects a nominal complement. From this perspective, it is anything but surprising that nonfinite (control) complementizers, both synchronically and diachronically, are so frequently prepositional in form and origin: the two functional categories share the [uD] feature (in addition to which, the complementizer bears a [uT] feature). This striking morphosyntactic overlap is an accident for most approaches to control, and would remain so even if the relevant feature on Fin were [+pred]/[+Op] (which are not defining features for prepositions anyway).

3.4   Logophoric Control

Recent years have seen intensive research on the syntax and semantics of attitude reports and logophoricity, which has produced some interesting and nontrivial results. These results have mostly been demonstrated in the realm of finite complementation to declarative and epistemic verbs; my goal in this section is to pursue their full implications for the analysis of OC. By its nature, this analysis will be highly integrative.[14]

In section 3.4.1, I survey the theoretical terrain of *de se* ascriptions, focusing on three types of mechanisms achieving them (indexical shift, local operator binding, and special *de re* ascriptions). In section 3.4.2, I summarize the arguments against the indexical shift view, and in section 3.4.3, I summarize the arguments against the local operator binding view. In section 3.4.4, I develop an analysis, in which the embedded C projects an argumental variable, bound by the controller and associated with a special *de re* description; this argument then saturates a predicative FinP projection, formed by PRO movement just as in predicative control. Further implications of this analysis for the interaction of OC with agreement are explored in section 3.5.

3.4.1   The Theoretical Terrain

Logophoric control is manifested in four classes of complements: propositional, factive, desiderative, and interrogative (see (5)). As shown in section 3.1, the predicates selecting these complements are attitude predicates.

(35) a. Mary claimed to have found the solution.
     b. Mary was shocked to find the solution.
     c. Mary intended to find the solution.
     d. Mary asked how to find the solution.

Note that only the factive complement, (35b), is entailed (being presupposed); the other complements are not. The attitude property reflects the fact that the evaluation of the complement crucially depends on the epistemic or bouletic state of the controller, Mary, over and above any physical or external conditions.

The embedded predicate enters a certain semantic relation with the controller, but unlike in predicative control, the relation is indirect. For example, (35c) does not entail that Mary found the solution; it entails only that she did so in those possible centered worlds in which her intentions come true (Chierchia 1984, Dowty 1985). More importantly, a specific interpretive condition holds to the effect that Mary's intention concerns her own self, and so would not be satisfied if she does not identify herself as participating in the intended event. This is the famous *de se* reading, which is often taken to be definitional of PRO in OC. As already discussed in section 3.2, this view is false—PRO in predicative control is not necessarily *de se*—and its falsity is a strong argument in favor of the minimal pronoun view of PRO. Is it true, though, that under predicates of logophoric control, PRO is obligatorily interpreted *de se*?

In reality, the situation is slightly more complex; it is summarized in (36).

(36) *Interpretations of OC PRO under attitude predicates*

Type	Subject control	Object control	
Examples	(*want, claim, wonder, plan, ...*)	Psychological verbs (*convince, persuade, dissuade, tempt, ...*)	Communicative verbs (*tell, ask, urge, recommend,...*)
Interpretation of PRO	Obligatory *de se*		Obligatory *de te*

While *de se* refers to the attitude holder's identification of himself for whom he is, *de te* refers to the attitude holder's identification of the addressee(s) for whom they are. The two senses are obviously related (and should receive a unified explanation), but the class of object control verbs splits between them, as originally noted by Chierchia (1990). Under an object Experiencer verb, PRO is understood *de se* with respect to the matrix object's perspective. Suppose Mary listens with John to a recording of a speech. The speaker in the recording is John himself, although he is not aware of that. After a while, Mary feels she has had enough and wants to put an end to it. (37a), which allows a *de re* reading, is a possible description of her actions, but (37b) is not, being obligatorily *de se*. The latter really implies something like the paraphrase in (37c).

(37) a. Mary persuaded John$_i$ that he$_i$ should shut up.
     b. Mary persuaded John to shut up.
     c. Mary caused John to entertain the desire: "I should shut up."

Now consider a verb of communication like *tell*, in the same scenario, only this time it is Mary who does not recognize the speaker of the recorded speech as the person standing next to her, John. Then we can describe her actions with (38a), in which *he* is read *de re*, but not with (38b), where PRO is obligatorily read *de te*. The latter must be paraphrased along the lines of (38c).

(38) a. Mary told John$_i$ that he$_i$ should shut up.
     b. Mary told John to shut up.
     c. Mary told John: "You should shut up."

Looking at table (36) from a θ-theoretic perspective, we can say that *de se* is triggered by Agent and Experiencer controllers and *de te* by Goal controllers. The semantic feature implicated in the former two and not in the latter is the presence of a mental state; in Reinhart's (2002) terms, *de se* is linked to [/+m] clusters. From the logophoric perspective, this natural class is defined by the AUTHOR coordinate of the embedded context: the matrix participant whose mental perspective is reported.[15]

Interestingly, in *de te* attitudes the link between the AUTHOR coordinate and control breaks. Quite clearly, Goal controllers need not entertain any mental state or attitude with respect to the embedded event. Furthermore, contrary to Stephenson's (2010) claim, it is not necessary that the Agent intend for the Goal to entertain an intention to perform the requested action. Because complements of object control always denote actions, and actions are intentional (see Jackendoff and Culicover 2003), the common interpretation of object control would indeed involve an intention on the part of the matrix object. But this is a fact about actions and not about the tacit intentions of the matrix Agent, who simply wants an action performed.

(39) a. Mary ordered John to stay home even if he doesn't want to.
     b. In meditation, the most dramatic results are achieved when you let go of your desires and intentions. When they reach this state, I tell my students to start the exercise.

What *de te* attitudes teach us, then, is that OC PRO (in attitude contexts) is not necessarily linked to the *de se* "center" in the world of evaluation—the attitude holder—as maintained in the centered-world approach (Stephenson 2010). The attitude holder *is* implicated, in fact, in fixing the worlds of evaluation, but need not be the controller. This in no way implies that PRO is ambiguous. Rather, there is a choice as to whether PRO is bound by the AUTHOR or the ADDRESSEE coordinate of the context of evaluation. This is the path I will take below. Nevertheless, since the bulk of the semantic work concentrates on explicating *de se* attitudes, the theoretical terrain is defined by the various ways this particular interpretation arises.

Building on the insights of the extensive work cited in note 14, I adopt two background assumptions, one about the syntax of attitude complements and one about their semantics. Syntactically, attitude verbs select clausal complements whose left periphery represents the context of speech (or thought) of the matrix event, also called the *context of evaluation*. This context is a tuple consisting of (at least) four coordinates: <AUTHOR,ADDRESSEE,TIME,WORLD>; to use Bianchi's (2003) apt term, it is the *logophoric center* of the clause. This information resides in the C head of the clause and may affect the interpretation of any context-sensitive element under the scope of C.[16] In section 3.4.4, I will actually suggest that the descriptive predicates AUTHOR and ADDRESSEE are not built into the context tuple but rather are introduced as presuppositional properties of the first two coordinates, which are simple variables, bound by the author and addressee of the matrix event. These variables may be projected as syntactic elements and carry nominal features (see below).

Semantically, the coordinates of the context of evaluation represent the way the attitude holder "locates" himself, his addressee, and the event time in the situations that express (conform to) his beliefs or desires. Thus, these are all *de se* (or *de te*) coordinates, although we will see shortly that there is more than one way in which the *de se* reading may arise.

Current research assumes that attitude verbs are intensional quantifiers but splits on the question of what they quantify over, and correlatively, what is the semantic type of their complements. One school of thought takes attitude complements to denote sets of contexts (Schlenker 2003, 2011, Anand and Nevins 2004, Anand 2006), whereas a second one takes them to denote properties or centered worlds (Chierchia 1990, Stephenson 2010, Pearson 2013). Within this space, there are three "paths to *de se*" in OC (see Anand 2006 for discussion).

(40) *Paths to* de se *in OC*
a. PRO is a shifted indexical.
b. PRO is locally bound by an operator (on a par with logophoric pronouns).
c. PRO triggers a special *de re* interpretation, which amounts to *de se*.

Path (40a) is represented in Anand and Nevins 2004, but the core intuition is already formulated in the appendix to Postal 1970 (see also Kuno 1972). As mentioned, it is also implicated in Schlenker's (2003) solution to the problem of forcing a *de se* presupposition in OC, and it seems to be lurking in Baker's (2008:131) analogy between English OC and indexical shift in Slave.[17] A formal representation of this analysis is given in (41), illustrated with the OC verb *intend*. Notice that the set of evaluated contexts in (41d) is selected in such a way that the author in each of them is the *de se* counterpart of the matrix subject.[18]

(41) *Semantics for OC verbs by indexical shift*
   a. $[\![\textit{[PRO to VP]}]\!]^{g,c,w} = \lambda c'.[\![\text{VP}]\!]^{g,c}(\text{AUTHOR}(c'))(c')$
   b. $[\![\textit{intend}]\!]^{g,c,w} = \lambda p.\lambda x.\lambda c'.\forall i' \in \text{INTEND}_{x,w}, p(i') = 1$
   c. $[\![\textit{intend [PRO to VP]}]\!]^{g,c,w} = \lambda x.\lambda c'.\forall i' \in \text{INTEND}_{x,w},$
      $[\![\text{VP}]\!]^{g,c}(\text{AUTHOR}(i'))(i') = 1$
   d. $\text{INTEND}_{x,w} = $ the set of contexts compatible with x's intentions in w

I discuss and eventually reject this analysis in section 3.4.2.

Path (40b) is represented in Chierchia 1990, von Stechow 2003, Anand 2006, Schlenker 2011, and Pearson 2013; it amounts to treating PRO as a logophor with the special property of being necessarily bound by the most local operator. The representation in (42) is adapted from Pearson 2013. Once again, notice how the *de se* reading is guaranteed by the way the set of individual-time-world tuples is selected, (42d).

(42) *Semantics for OC verbs by local operator binding*
   a. $\textit{[PRO to VP]}]\!]^{g,c} = \lambda z.\lambda t'.\lambda w'.[\![\text{VP}]\!]^{g,c}(z)(t')(w')$
   b. $[\![\textit{intend}]\!]^{g,c} = \lambda P.\lambda x.\lambda t.\lambda w.\forall <w',t',y> \in \text{INTEND}_{x,t,w}, \exists t'': t' <_{\text{precedes}} t''$
      $\& \ P(y)(t'')(w')$
   c. $[\![\textit{intend [PRO to VP]}]\!]^{g,c} = \lambda x.\lambda t.\lambda w.\forall <w',t',y> \in \text{INTEND}_{x,t,w} , \exists t'':$
      $t' <_{\text{precedes}} t'' \ \& \ [\![\text{VP}]\!]^{g,c}(y)(t'')(w')$
   d. $\text{INTEND}_{x,t,w} = \{<x,t,w> |$ it is compatible with what x intends
      in w at t for x to be y in w' and for t to be t'$\}$

I discuss the shortcomings of this line of research in section 3.4.3.

Path (42c) is represented in Schlenker 2003 and Maier 2011. As the philosophical literature on *de re* attitudes makes clear, the range of *de re* ascriptions is very broad, the only constraint being that the description of the *res* must stand in some "acquaintance relation" to the attitude holder. In this context, it is possible to view *de se* as that special case of *de re* where the acquaintance relation that holds between the attitude holder and the *res* is identity ("This person is me!"). Crucially, on this analysis only, but not on the other two analyses, PRO is directly bound by the controller. This difference will play an important role in the explanation of the OC-NC generalization in section 3.5.

The "special *de re*" analysis, however, faces difficulties with obligatory *de se* elements, like PRO in attitude contexts. The standard procedure is to attach a lexical presupposition to the *de se* element, to the effect that the only accessible acquaintance relation is the identity relation. This is carried out by a shifted indexical feature in Schlenker 2003 (effectively blending (40b) and (40c)) and by a pragmatically interpreted feature in Maier 2011. Neither solution is compatible with the principal constraint of the present study—the analysis of PRO as a minimal pronoun (see section 3.2)—and both would need to multiply the lexical entries for PRO in other environments. The problem may be merely implementational, however: perhaps PRO in attitude contexts is the same minimal pronoun, and the *de se* presupposition is introduced by a distinct element in the structure. This is the path I will explore in section 3.4.4.

3.4.2 OC PRO Is Not a Shifted Indexical

To start from Postal's (1970) original insight, control complements represent indirect discourse reporting direct discourse events. When the "underlying" direct discourse sentence is recovered, a personal pronoun emerges as its subject.

(43) a. Harry told Betty to marry him/(You) marry me, Harry told Betty.
　　b. Harry asked Betty to marry him/Will you (please) marry me, Harry asked Betty.
　　c. Harry promised Betty to leave/I will leave, Harry promised Mary.
　　d. Harry asked Betty when to leave/When should I leave, Harry asked Betty.

Postal stated the generalization: If the direct discourse subject is 2nd person, the indirect discourse subject (PRO) is object-controlled; if the direct discourse subject is 1st person, the indirect discourse subject is subject-controlled. Note that the semantics of personal pronouns guarantees the correct *de se* and *de te* interpretations, if direct discourse does underlie indirect discourse.

As it turns out, certain environments in certain languages wear their direct discourse complements on their sleeves: a 1st person pronoun in a complement of an attitude verb refers not to the speaker but to the attitude holder (often the matrix subject), and a 2nd person pronoun in the complement refers to the addressee of the attitude (the matrix object). An example from Zazaki is given in (44) (Anand and Nevins 2004); note that the embedded subject may refer either to the speaker (index k) or to *Hesen* (index j).[19]

(44) Hɛseni$_j$　(mɨ-ra)　va　kɛ　ɛz$_{j/k}$　dɛwletia.
　　Hesen.OBL　(I.OBL-to)　said　that　I　rich.BE.PRES
　　'Hesen said that {I am, Hesen is} rich.'

The formal analysis of this phenomenon involves overwriting the *context* parameter of evaluation (a tuple consisting of the world, time, location, author, and addressee of the utterance context) with the *index* parameter (a similar tuple corresponding to the attitude context). Thus, within the worlds of evaluation for the complement in (44)—all the worlds consistent with what Hesen says—the 1st person pronoun refers to the "author" of the world, namely, to Hesen. Indexical shift is a shift in the context of evaluation, triggered by specific verbs (or pronouns; see below).

Anand and Nevins (2004) suggest that OC PRO should be simply identified with a shifted indexical, as in (45) (where c is the constant context of evaluation and i is the current, shiftable context of evaluation).

(45) a. $[\![PRO_{subj}]\!]^{c,i} = \text{AUTHOR}(i)$ *subject-controlled PRO*
      b. $[\![PRO_{obj}]\!]^{c,i} = \text{ADDRESSEE}(i)$ *object-controlled PRO*

The proposal to be developed in section 3.4.4 will end up semantically equivalent to indexical shift. Crucially, however, it will not make use of the idea that PRO is an indexical pronoun. There are, in fact, serious objections to this idea.

The first objection, possibly minor, is that on the indexical shift theory, one must posit two entries for OC PRO, (45a) and (45b), just as one must distinguish the lexical entries of *I* and *you*. Together with nonindexical PRO (used in predicative, nonattitude contexts), this makes for three types of PRO—three times as many as needed on the minimal pronoun approach.

The second objection concerns crosslinguistic distribution. The phenomenon of shifted indexicals is rather uncommon; to date it has been documented in around ten languages (see note 19). Moreover, in most of them, indexical shift is restricted to the complement of a single verb, 'say', or possibly three or four verbs. In Slave, it is found with 'say', 'tell', and two versions of 'think/ want'; and in Navajo, it is found with 'say' for all speakers and dialectically with 'think' and 'want'. Whatever one's favorite mechanism of deriving shifted indexicals, it has to be a highly marked one.

But then the question arises: what makes this mechanism completely mundane in the realm of control, available in most languages of the world and for dozens of verbs in each language? In fact, none of the complement clauses in which genuine indexical shift has been documented displays OC; they are all uncontrolled complements. These asymmetries are puzzling if PRO is just another type of shifted indexical, albeit an unpronounced one.[20]

The third objection concerns selectivity and optionality. Even within the small data set of shifted indexicals documented in the literature, there is a great deal of variation. In Slave, 1st person pronouns obligatorily shift under 'say' but only optionally shift under 'want'; 2nd person pronouns do not shift under these verbs. On the other hand, both 1st and 2nd person pronouns optionally shift under 'tell'. The latter pattern is also exhibited by 'say' in Amharic and Navajo. In Zazaki, shifting is optional too (under 'say'), but it is unselective (all indexicals may shift).

The literature accounts for this variation by assuming that the presence of context-shifting operators in the complement clause is regulated by largely idiosyncratic selectional specifications (Anand 2006, Baker 2008, Schlenker 2011). Turning to OC, however, we witness striking systematicity: all verbs with Agent/Experiencer controllers, we would have to assume, induce obligatory shift of the 1st person PRO, and all verbs with Goal controllers induce obligatory shift of the 2nd person PRO (see table (36)). Appropriate selectional specifications can no doubt be tailored for OC complements, but this would beg the question of what makes indexical shift so systematic in OC but not elsewhere.

The fourth and final objection concerns simple morphological facts. Genuine shifted indexicals preserve their "direct discourse" [person] value; thus, the embedded subject in (44) is specified [person:1]. OC PRO, in contrast, inherits its [person] value from the controller, regardless of its interpretation as a "shifted" indexical. This can be observed on agreeing reflexives.

(46) a. John planned [PRO to promote himself/*myself].
     b. John planned: "I will promote myself."

This mismatch between the form and semantic value of OC PRO in attitude contexts is a well-recognized problem (see the extensive discussion in Schlenker 2003), but it is particularly thorny for the indexical shift theory, since on this theory, PRO is *inherently specified* as the context's author or addressee, just as the pronouns *I* and *you* are. To reconcile these facts, one would have to maintain that only in the case of shifted indexicals (but not in the case of unshifted ones) are [person] features semantically interpreted but morphologically unspecified, and that a separate process of agreement (with the controller) guarantees their morphological valuation. This is possible in principle, but surely less appealing than the null hypothesis, whereby PRO is inherently unspecified both semantically and morphologically.

To summarize this section: there are compelling theoretical and empirical reasons to reject solution (40a) to the obligatory *de se* interpretation of OC PRO (in attitude complements). I next consider solution (40b), local binding by an operator.

3.4.3 OC PRO Is Not a Logophoric Pronoun
The term *logophoric control* naturally brings to mind the familiar phenomenon of logophoric pronouns (LPs), studied extensively in African languages; it is occasionally extended to cover long-distance reflexives as well (see Culy 1994

and Reuland 2006 for useful surveys). Indeed, there are two obvious similarities between PRO in attitude contexts and LPs: (i) both occur only in attitude complements, and (ii) both are bound by participants of the speech/thought event. The examples in (47) are from Edo (Baker 2008:135) and Ewe (Clements 1975); notice that the embedded logophoric pronouns are obligatorily coindexed with their matrix antecedents, which, in turn, determine the AUTHOR coordinate of the embedded context.

(47) a. *Edo*

    Òzò   miàmián   wẹ̀ẹ̀ írèn   kìé   èkhù.

    Ozo   forgot   that he.LOG opened door

    'Ozo$_i$ forgot that he$_{i/*k}$ opened the door.'

  b. *Ewe*

    Me-se tso   Kofi gbɔ be   yè-xɔ   nuana.

    I-hear from Kofi side that he.LOG-receive gift

    'I heard from Kofi$_i$ that he$_{i/*k}$ received a gift.'

There is strong evidence that LPs are licensed by operators located at the CP periphery (Koopman and Sportiche 1989, Safir 2004, Adesola 2005, Anand 2006, Baker 2008). It is therefore not implausible to suggest that OC PRO is a special kind of logophoric pronoun (von Stechow 2003, Anand 2006). There are problems with this assimilation, however, both within the present framework and independently of it, similar in nature to the problems with the analysis of OC PRO as a shifted indexical.

    First, in terms of distribution, LPs are found in complements of declarative and cognitive verbs but *never inside OC complements* (Culy 1994). This absence of overlap is puzzling on the view that the same operator that licenses LPs also licenses OC PRO.

    Second, logophoric domains are often optional. Although certain languages employ designated complementizers that force the use of LPs in their scope (if reference to a matrix argument is desired), the more common pattern is for attitude complements to display optional logophoricity effects. Of course, this is unlike OC PRO (under attitude verbs), which is obligatorily anchored to the embedded context.

    Third, among the potential antecedents for LPs (in various languages) is the discourse role SOURCE (see Sells 1987), as in (47b); but to the best of my knowledge, this role is never assumed by OC controllers.

    Fourth, whereas OC PRO must be bound by the most local operator, LPs need not be locally bound and in fact may pick as their binder any c-commanding complementizer (capable of licensing LPs), however distant it is. Moreover, clausemate LPs need not be bound by the same operator.

Fifth, LPs are not restricted to subject position, but PRO is.

Sixth, just as with the indexical shift theory of OC, the mechanism of agreement between PRO and the controller is unclear. While PRO must inherit the ϕ-features of its local binder—the individual abstractor located in the embedded C—owing to the binding relation (Heim 2008, Kratzer 2009; see (69) below), how is the latter guaranteed to inherit the ϕ-features of the matrix controller? Crucially, no *syntactic* relation is established between the variable y and the abstractor λx in the formula (42c); they are only linked by the "*de se* counterpart" relation in the lexical semantics of the control verb. While it is customary in the semantic literature to take that as sufficient grounds for morphological agreement (see, e.g., von Stechow 2003), the causal relation is stipulated, not explained by any known syntactic or morphological procedure.[21]

All these considerations suggest that analyzing PRO as a locally bound pronoun (possibly with a [log] feature) would still leave us far behind the goal of explaining its properties and distribution. From the present perspective of attempting to unify all the manifestations of OC PRO, this analysis would also be unappealing for an independent reason: it cannot extend to predicative control (where no logophoric effects exist) and hence would be forced to posit two types of PRO, failing to meet the minimal pronoun desideratum. Although the investigation of LPs holds many important insights for the analysis of logophoric control, the latter cannot be reduced to the former.[22]

3.4.4 The Proposal: Binding a Coordinate of C

Having considered and dismissed two types of analyses—PRO is a shifted indexical or a logophoric pronoun—I can now present my proposal: PRO is linked to a variable bound by the matrix controller, which is associated with a special *de re* description (the "authorship" relation). In this section, I lay out the formal syntactic and semantic ingredients of this analysis.[23] I then discuss the morphological aspects in section 3.5, where a novel, independent argument for favoring this proposal over its alternatives will come to light.

Recall that on the view of attitude verbs as quantifiers over sets of contexts, a context is taken to be a tuple of coordinates, which are nothing but variables, each associated with its own indexical descriptive content: i = <AUTHOR(i), ADDRESSEE(i),TIME(i),WORLD(i)>. We may think of the coordinates of i (the embedded context) as *arguments* of C (the complementizer). While these arguments are normally not present in the syntax (being implicit, so to speak), they may project syntactically under certain circumstances. This is the fate of the AUTHOR (or ADDRESSEE) coordinate in OC.

It is worth noting that nothing forces this particular packaging of the coordinate variables with their respective descriptive contents. Semantically, an equivalent result could be achieved if the context consisted of pure variables, bound by the matrix attitude holder and addressee, with their descriptive content being introduced syntagmatically, so to speak. This is the intuition I will explore below, at least for the individual coordinates, leaving open the question whether the TIME and WORLD coordinates should be treated the same way. Thus, I take the context introduced by an attitude predicate to be i = <x,y,TIME(i),WORLD(i)>. The individual variables x and y are directly bound by the arguments denoting attitude holder and addressee in the matrix clause. Importantly, this binding relation is inherent in the semantics of any attitude verb and is not particular to OC environments. What is special about the OC complementizer (henceforth, C^{OC}) are two properties: (i) syntactically, it must project one of its individual coordinates as a specifier; (ii) semantically, it introduces the "special *de re*" presupposition of an identity acquaintance relation, which amounts to an obligatory *de se* reading.

Before I turn to OC as a special case of *de re* ascription, let me outline the general case. The formal implementation below is an adaptation of the proposal in Percus and Sauerland 2003a (see also Pearson 2013:chap. 7); for discussion of the background philosophical and semantic issues arising with *de re* beliefs, see Percus and Sauerland 2003a,b, as well as Schlenker 2003, 2011 and Anand 2006.

On the *de re* analysis, a sentence like *Ralph believes that Ortcutt is a spy* is rendered as 'There is a vivid description of Ortcutt for Ralph such that under this description, Ralph believes of Ortcutt that he is a spy'. The two notable features of this analysis are that (i) the attitude verb selects an additional (syntactically invisible) argument, the so-called *res* of the belief; and (ii) the acquaintance relation between the attitude holder (AH) and the *res* must be unique and "vivid"—which means, at least, that the AH must consciously associate the description with the *res*. I will follow Anand (2006) in calling this cognitive condition the *suitability condition* on *de re* beliefs. Importantly, the suitability condition implies that an egocentric perspective (of the AH) is built even into standard *de re* beliefs. This will be the key to the "*de se* as a special *de re*" analysis, in which the AH is suitably acquainted with a *res* that happens to be himself.

Following Percus and Sauerland (2003), I will introduce the *unique acquaintance* relation between the AH and the *res* via a concept generator, G, defined in (48).

(48) $[\![G]\!]^{g,c} = \lambda res_e.\lambda i'_\kappa.\iota(r_e)$: r is picked out by the description G of the *res* for the AH (= the AH's concept of the *res*) in context i'.

One may think of G as a way of picking out the "counterpart" of the *res* in the AH's doxastic alternatives. Note that I treat concept generators as functions from individual-*context* pairs (as in Anand 2006) and not from individual-*world* pairs (as in Percus and Sauerland 2003a), in order to be able to define Gs that pick out specific coordinates of the context as the description of the *res*. I do follow Percus and Sauerland in assuming that the acquaintance relation must be unique. Given (48), *suitability* can be defined as follows:

(49) A concept generator is *suitable* for an attitude holder x in context c if and only if:
    a. *Acquaintance:* $\forall y \in Dom(G)$, x is acquainted with y in c.
    b. *Uniqueness:* $\forall y,z \in Dom(G)$, $y \neq z \rightarrow G(y) \neq G(z)$.

Finally, to capture the fact that *de re* beliefs are relativized to descriptions, the attitude complement is analyzed as a function from concept generators to propositions (the variable *Q* below). The proposition itself is produced by predicating the embedded property of the "counterpart" of the *res*; below, this embedded property is the denotation of the same FinP used in predicative control, and the *res* counterpart is introduced as a nominal argument of C, a transitive head just like Fin.

The different pieces are put together in (50)–(51). In (50), GP is the counterpart of *res* in i' under G.

(50) De re: *The general case*

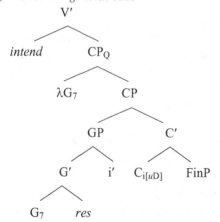

(51) a. $[\![CP]\!]^{g,c} = \lambda i'.[\![FinP]\!]^{g,c}(g(7)(res)(i'))(i')$

    b. $[\![CP_Q]\!]^{g,c} = \lambda G_7.\lambda i'.[\![FinP]\!]^{g,c}(G_7(res)(i'))(i')$

    c. $[\![intend]\!]^{g,c} = \lambda Q.\lambda res.\lambda x.\lambda w.\exists G$ for x in w $\wedge$ G is suitable
      $\wedge\ \forall i'\in INTEND_{x,w},\ Q(G)(i')=1$

    d. $[\![[intend\ CP_Q]\!]^{g,c} = \lambda res.\lambda x.\lambda w.\exists G$ for x in w $\wedge$ G is suitable
      $\wedge\ \forall i'\in INTEND_{x,w},\ [\![FinP]\!]^{g,c}(G(res)(i'))(i')=1$

For example, *Ralph intended for Betty to join the club* receives the paraphrase 'There is a concept generator for Ralph that establishes a suitable acquaintance relation between Ralph and Betty under some description, and in all of the contexts that conform to Ralph's intentions, the person picked by that description joins the club'.

Our interest is in reflexive *de re* beliefs, in which *res* = AH (the variable x in (51)).

(52) For *res* = AH (G is a description of the attitude holder for himself):
    $[\![[intend\ CP_Q]\!]^{g,c} = \lambda x.\lambda w.\exists G$ for x in w $\wedge$ G is suitable
    $\wedge\ \forall i'\in INTEND_{x,w},\ [\![FinP]\!]^{g,c}(G(x)(i'))(i')=1$

Note that this need not generate a *de se* reading. $G(x)(i')$ could be 'the person x sees in the mirror in i'', consistent with a misidentification scenario. To guarantee the *de se* reading, we need to define G_{SELF}. Similarly, for *de te* readings we define G_{THOU}.

(53) a. $G_{SELF} =_{def} G: \forall y\in Dom(G), G(y) = $ AUTHOR
      $[\![G_{SELF}]\!]^{g,c}(z) = \lambda c'.$AUTHOR$(c')$

    b. $G_{THOU} =_{def} G: \forall y\in Dom(G), G(y) = $ ADDRESSEE
      $[\![G_{THOU}]\!]^{g,c}(z) = \lambda c'.$ADDRESSEE$(c')$

G_{SELF} and G_{THOU} are constant functions. Because of the uniqueness condition (49b) on suitable Gs, their domains are singletons. Thus, every individual is paired with a unique G_{SELF} and a unique G_{THOU}, which map it to the AUTHOR and ADDRESSEE functions, respectively. Focusing on *de se*, it is easy to see that the AUTHOR function yields it. In the general terms of *de re* beliefs, if one of the suitable concept generators for AH is G_{SELF}, then AH is known to himself as the author of his thoughts.

The crucial question is what makes *de se* obligatory in OC contexts. From the present perspective, this translates to the question, What forces the choice of G_{SELF} among all the possible Gs? This bit of semantic information cannot be part of the meaning of the attitude verb itself, which, of course, accommodates all kinds of *de re* ascriptions, not just the special case of *de se* (see (51)). Rather, the natural locus for this information is the OC complementizer, C^{OC}; it is only in combination with this complementizer that attitude verbs generate obligatory *de se* readings. This intuition is rendered below as a presupposition triggered by C^{OC}.

Syntactically, logophoric OC complements instantiate the general scheme of *de re* complements (50). The predicative FinP is exactly the constituent formed in predicative control (see (32)). Recall that this constituent is a derived predicate formed by PRO movement to Spec,Fin. In logophoric control, it serves as the complement of the complementizer that hosts the logophoric center. In this way, the two types of control are strongly integrated; in effect, logophoric control is a logophoric center overlaid, as a second tier, on predicative control, the first tier.[24]

The difference lies in what the predicate is predicated of. Whereas FinP is directly predicated of the matrix controller in predicative control, in logophoric control it is predicated of GP, a function of a projected coordinate of the embedded context. This coordinate is nothing but a *de re* variable bound by the controller and associated with a *de se* interpretation thanks to a "G_{SELF} presupposition" triggered by C^{OC}. Keeping to devices already utilized in the analysis of predicative control, assume that the presence of this syntactic argument in Spec,CP is forced by selection. Just like Fin, C^{OC} is a transitive head endowed with a selectional feature, $[uD]$. This feature forces one of the nominal coordinates of the embedded context i′—corresponding to the AH or addressee—to project as the specifier of C, turning the complement into what one might call a "perspectival CP."

On minimal assumptions, this coordinate is nothing but a pure variable—hence, I suggest, is realized as a minimal pronoun too, just like PRO, consisting of the feature bundle $[D,\phi:]$ (see (28)). In section 3.5, I return to the mechanism by which the ϕ-features of this element are valued. To keep the symbols distinct, I will refer to a projected AUTHOR coordinate as *pro*$_x$ and to a projected ADDRESSEE coordinate as *pro*$_y$.

The central player in logophoric control, then, is C^{OC}, which performs four functions: (i) it projects one of its individual coordinate variables as a specifier, (ii) it predicates its complement of (a function of) this variable, (iii) it attaches a G_{SELF} presupposition to this variable, and (iv) it abstracts over contexts. Note that of these functions, only the first and the third are specific to C^{OC}, the other two being shared by all complementizers that mediate *de re* attitudes.

Diagram (54) illustrates the syntactic derivation of a simple attitude subject control sentence, *John intends to visit Athens*. Object control receives a parallel treatment, except that $C_i{}'$ projects *pro*$_y$ instead of *pro*$_x$. *pro*$_y$ would be associated with G_{SELF} under psychological object control and with G_{THOU} under communicative object control (see (36)–(38)).

(54) *Derivation of logophoric control*

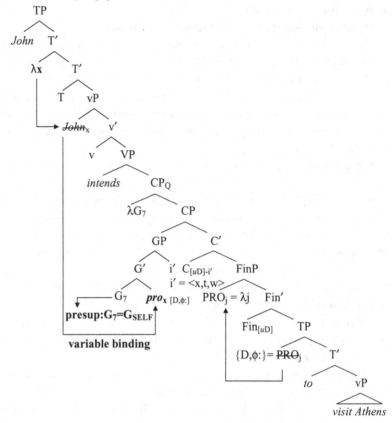

Five distinctive advantages of this analysis merit comment. First, this analysis sides with proposals in Chierchia 1990, Anand 2006, Schlenker 2011, and Pearson 2013, and against proposals in Schlenker 2003, von Stechow 2003, and Stephenson 2010, in that the binding relation into which PRO enters is represented *syntactically*; the bindee *pro*$_x$ occupies a position in the syntactic tree and not just in the semantic formulae. There is, in fact, diverse evidence that operators regulating logophoricity, point of view, and context shifting are part of syntax, interacting with binding, scope, and agreement phenomena (see Koopman and Sportiche 1989, Uriagereka 1995, Bianchi 2003, Safir 2004, Speas 2004, Anand 2006, Baker 2008, Sigurðsson 2011, Sundaresan 2012, Haegeman and Hill 2013, Shklovsky and Sudo 2014). In section 3.5, I present a novel argument for the syntactic reality of the local binder of PRO, drawing on its interaction with agreement (the OC-NC generalization).[25]

Second, the *de se* component is dissociated from PRO, still a minimal pronoun just as it is in predicative control. This adequately captures the cross-linguistic observation that obligatory *de se* is a property of attitude OC complements per se and not an exclusive feature of PRO. Thus, controlled lexical pronouns in Korean (Madigan 2008a) and Hungarian (Szabolcsi 2009) exhibit this property just as PRO does in the same environments (I return in chapter 5 to controlled pronouns). Conversely, PRO fails to exhibit it in nonattitude contexts (see (25), (26c–d), (27)). The property only arises in attitude OC complements because it is specifically written into the lexical entry of their head, C^{OC}. It arises as a presupposition attached to an argument of the head, just as run-of-the-mill lexical presuppositions do.

Third, note that the effect of the transitivity of C—its selectional feature [uD]—is to force control by *one* of the two individual coordinates (AUTHOR or ADDRESSEE) without specifying which (setting aside split control; see chapter 5). Another way of putting it is that the "control module"—the procedure for selecting a matrix controller—is not part of the LF of logophoric control structures. This neutrality is a virtue, because it is well-known that control may shift from the matrix subject to the matrix object and vice versa, under complex semantic and pragmatic conditions (see section 4.3). The current division of labor correctly situates the negotiation between the two options in post-LF interpretive processes.

Fourth, the analysis derives in a principled way a property of OC that used to baffle semanticists: the fact that PRO (or the context variable associated with it) is necessarily bound by the most local operator (Chierchia 1990, von Stechow 2003, Anand 2006, Schlenker 2011). Within the semantic approaches, this locality is achieved by brute force: "tagging" PRO and its binder with the same diacritic or imposing some ad hoc condition on its context variable. Nothing of that sort is needed on the analysis in (54). PRO is locally bound by pro_x (itself a variable, not an operator) because the former creates the predicate that applies to the latter. Furthermore, the context variable to which the G_{SELF} function applies must be the local i′ (and not, say, the matrix c*) because the function is *introduced* by C_i.[26]

Fifth, the explanation for the subjecthood of PRO and the ban on lexical subjects in predicative control readily carries over to the present case of logophoric control. pro_x binds the open position in the predicative FinP, which, as discussed in section 3.3, must be the subject position (because of locality). And a lexical DP instead of or in addition to PRO would produce a proposition (see (33)) that would fail to combine with pro_x via predication.

At this point, it is possible to provide an explicit compositional semantics for logophoric OC, on the basis of the lexical entry for *intend* in (51c) and the structure in (54).

(55) *Semantic composition of logophoric control*

    a. $[\![[_{\text{FinP}}\ \text{PRO to visit Athens}]\!]^{g,c} = \lambda z.\lambda c'.[\![\text{visit Athens}]\!]^{g,c}(z)(c')$

    b. $[\![C_{i'}^{OC}]\!]^{g,c} = G_7 = G_{\text{SELF}}: \lambda P.\lambda y.\lambda i'.P(y)(i')=1$

    c. $[\![C']\!]^{g,c} = [\![C_{i'}^{OC}]\!]^{g,c}([\![\text{FinP}]\!]^{g,c}) = \lambda y.\lambda i'.G_7 = G_{\text{SELF}}: [\![\text{visit Athens}]\!]^{g,c}(y)$
       $(i')=1$

    d. $[\![GP]\!]^{g,c} = g(7)(g(x))(i')$

    e. $[\![CP]\!]^{g,c} = [\![C'^{g,c}([\![GP]\!]^{g,c}) =$
       $\lambda i'.G_7 = G_{\text{SELF}}: [\![\text{visit Athens}]\!]^{g,c}(g(7)(g(x))(i'))(i')=1 =$
       $\lambda i'.G_7 = G_{\text{SELF}}: [\![\text{visit Athens}]\!]^{g,c}(G_{\text{SELF}}(g(x))(i'))(i')=1$

    f. $[\![CP_Q]\!]^{g,c} = \lambda G_7\ [\![CP]\!]^{g,c} = \lambda G_7.\lambda i'.G_7 = G_{\text{SELF}}:$
       $[\![\text{visit Athens}]\!]^{g,c}(G_{\text{SELF}}(g(x))(i'))(i')=1$

    g. $[\![intend]\!]^{g,c} = \lambda Q.\lambda x.\lambda w.\exists G$ for x in w $\wedge$ G is suitable $\wedge$
       $\forall i' \in \text{INTEND}_{x,w},\ Q(G)(i')=1$

    h. $[\![[intend\ CP_Q]]\!]^{g,c} = \lambda x.\lambda w.G = G_{\text{SELF}}: \exists G$ for x in w $\wedge$ G is suitable
       $\wedge\ \forall i' \in \text{INTEND}_{x,w},\ [\![\text{visit Athens}]\!]^{g,c}(G_{\text{SELF}}(g(x))(i'))(i')=1$

The existential quantification over G is superfluous, given that its value is fixed as G_{SELF}, yielding (55i). Since there is always a suitable choice of G_{SELF}, (55i) is simplified as (55j); and since G_{SELF} maps its argument to AUTHOR, we obtain (55k).

(55) i. $= \lambda x.\lambda w.G_{\text{SELF}}$ is suitable $\wedge\ \forall i' \in \text{INTEND}_{x,w},$
       $[\![\text{visit Athens}]\!]^{g,c}(G_{\text{SELF}}(g(x))(i'))(i')=1$

    j. $= \lambda x.\lambda w.\forall i' \in \text{INTEND}_{x,w},\ [\![\text{visit Athens}]\!]^{g,c}(G_{\text{SELF}}(g(x))(i'))(i')=1$

    k. $= \lambda x.\lambda w.\forall i' \in \text{INTEND}_{x,w},\ [\![\text{visit Athens}]\!]^{g,c}(\text{AUTHOR}(i'))(i')=1$

(55k) adequately captures the obligatory *de se* reading of logophoric OC (cf. (41c)).[27] Consider an AH who is the *de-se*-violating amnesiac. The *res* = AH, who performs the embedded action, does *not* fall under the description "author of my thoughts." And so there would be contexts i' in which AUTHOR(i'), the person AH takes himself to be in i', does not visit Athens. This would make the sentence false, as desired. We thus derive the right semantics for logophoric control on the basis of a general analysis of *de re* attitudes.

Left to be explained is the mechanism by which PRO comes to agree in ϕ-features with the controller. I now turn to this question.

3.5 Agreement with the Controller

The same syntactic structures that support predicative and logophoric control also support the agreement relations manifested in these constructions. In this section, I lay out the mechanisms of agreement involved in both situations.

Understanding these mechanisms will pave the way to understanding why they interact differently with morphological inflection in the controlled clause (the OC-NC generalization), the topic of section 3.6.

In line with a growing body of research, I assume that agreement processes take place at PF (see Sigurðsson 2006, 2009, Bobaljik 2008, Chung to appear, Landau to appear). This assumption captures the traditional insight that agreement itself—the insertion of inflectional morphology that registers the interpretable φ-features of a nominal elsewhere in the sentence—does not have semantic effects; apparent counterexamples are indeed rare and plausibly involve interpreting "hidden" material rather than the inflectional morphology itself. The uninterpretability of agreement accounts straightforwardly for the common observation that utterances have the same semantic import in dialects that differ in their agreement properties as well as in agreement-less languages. It also explains how purely morphological processes can condition the operation of agreement, as documented in the sources cited above.

Because PF, at least prior to linearization, operates on fully syntactic configurations, agreement may perfectly be subject to structural constraints (c-command, locality, etc.). However, because PF does not communicate with LF, agreement outcomes may not have semantic consequences. This point is important to bear in mind when we discuss the valuation of PRO below.

Let us now turn to predicative control. It is well-known that syntactic predication is a configuration of agreement: if the predicate bears any φ-features, they normally match the φ-features of the subject. Matching is achieved in one of two ways: (i) feature transmission from subject to predicate, or (ii) feature transmission from predicate to subject. An example of case (i) is adjectival agreement (56a); an example of case (ii) is verbal agreement with *pro*, which is likely inserted as a minimal pronoun with unvalued features (56b). (i) and (ii) instantiate *dependent* agreement; I turn to independent agreement below.[28]

(56) a. *Hebrew*
ha-yelad-im   smex-im.
the-child-PL.M happy-PL.M

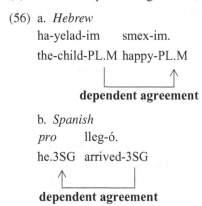

dependent agreement

b. *Spanish*
pro   lleg-ó.
he.3SG   arrived-3SG

dependent agreement

Classical GB-style Spec-head agreement is capable of yielding agreement in these two cases. Alternatively, they may be handled by the more current operation Agree, which transmits φ-values from valued to unvalued occurrences of features. The choice between these options is not crucial for present concerns.

Let us see how this type of agreement is instantiated in predicative control. Recall that a FinP projection is turned into a predicate by the movement of an operator PRO to its specifier. This predicate then applies to the controller DP via some predicative head (Rel or light v). Agreement thus piggybacks two syntactic dependencies here: movement and predication.

(57) *φ-agreement in predicative control*

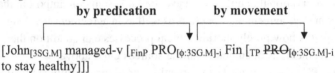

[John[3SG.M] managed-v [FinP PRO[φ:3SG.M]-i Fin [TP ~~PRO~~[φ:3SG.M]-i to stay healthy]]]

The operator PRO is generated as a minimal pronoun; its [φ:] bundle is valued at PF by the saturating DP controller, *John*. This step could be the result of a direct Agree (*John*,PRO) operation, or the indirect result of a prior Agree (*John*,Fin) operation. Either way, the phase-edge position of the raised PRO and Fin guarantees the locality and the success of this step (Polinsky 2003, Bobaljik and Wurmbrand 2005). The φ-values transmitted to the raised PRO are shared by its lower copy, the variable PRO, by virtue of the movement chain (on feature sharing, see Pesetsky and Torrego 2007).

Consider now how agreement works in logophoric control. Recall that FinP is embedded under a perspectival CP that encodes the matrix participants. The head of this CP projects a pronominal variable, which simultaneously saturates the FinP predicate and is bound by the matrix controller. Thus, agreement travels along three syntactic dependencies: variable binding, predication, and movement.

(58) *φ-agreement in logophoric control*

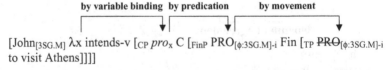

[John[3SG.M] λx intends-v [CP *pro*x C [FinP PRO[φ:3SG.M]-i Fin [TP ~~PRO~~[φ:3SG.M]-i to visit Athens]]]]

The added component in (58), compared to (57), is variable binding. That variable binding serves as a vehicle for feature transmission has been forcefully argued by Heim (2008) and Kratzer (2009). In particular, even [person] features become semantically vacuous in contexts of variable binding and lose their indexical presuppositions. The examples in (59) support a sloppy reading in which the pronoun *my* is interpreted as a (possessive) variable ranging over all the individuals in the comparison set and not just over the speaker.

(59) a. Only I did my homework.
b. I am the only one who takes care of my children.

Both Heim and Kratzer propose that bound variables inherit their φ-features from their binders *at PF*. Because those features are not present in the syntax— rather, only a minimal pronoun is—they are not visible to semantic interpreta- tion.[29] This PF view of agreement has interesting consequences for partial control as well, which I explore in Landau to appear. Combined with my earlier claims about standard agreement, it yields a unified conclusion: *all* φ-valuation, whether by Agree or by Feature Transmission under variable binding, occurs at PF.[30]

So far, then, we have seen that the proposed analysis of predicative and logophoric control, motivated on syntactic and semantic grounds, accounts rather smoothly for the fact that PRO agrees with the controller. The fact that we need only appeal to mechanisms of agreement already established inde- pendently of control is encouraging.

There is, however, one difference between the working of agreement in predication and its working in variable binding, which proves crucial for what follows. The difference is stated in (60).

(60) *Agreement in predication and variable binding*
a. The formation of a predication relation is *not* contingent on feature matching between the subject and the predicate.
b. The formation of a variable binding relation *is* contingent on feature matching between the binder and the pronominal variable.

Beginning with (60a), notice that predication is closely related with agreement only with verbal and adjectival predicates. PP predicates bear no φ-features, and nominal predicates need not match their subjects in φ-features.

(61) a. John is [$_{PP}$ out of his mind].
b. Those women[$_{PL.F}$] are [$_{DP}$ a committee]$_{[SG.NEUT]}$.

Baker (2008) argues that nominal predications never involve syntactic agree- ment; both the subject and the predicate are generated with independent fea- tures and apparent matching effects are solely the result of semantic consis- tency.[31] We may concur with Baker that nominal predicates are inherently specified for φ-features while still allowing a process of independent agree- ment to apply, if possible, and under restricted conditions (cf. (56)).

(62) These women[PL.F] are actresses[PL.F].

independent agreement

Importantly, (62) involves feature *matching*, not feature transmission. Feature matching between an independently valued predicative head and its subject is also assumed by Kratzer (2009) in the analysis of examples like (59b). That predication as such does not depend on Feature Transmission can even be seen with adjectival predicates that fail to agree with their subjects. Such is the well-known case of Icelandic quirky constructions like (63) (from Sigurðsson 2008).

(63) *Icelandic*
      Henni er kalt/*köld/*kaldri.
      she.DAT is cold.NOM.SG.NEUT/*NOM.SG.F/*DAT.SG.F
      'She is cold.'

What emerges from these observations is that the formation of the predicative relation itself is not contingent on feature transmission. This is not to say that agreement is always optional under predication. Clearly, when the predicate is not inherently specified for a given ϕ-value, it must undergo valuation; by assumption, unvalued ϕ-features are morphologically illicit and tolerated only as a last resort ("default agreement") if no potential ϕ-source is around. Thus, plural agreement in (56a) is mandatory; however, it is mandatory not because of some general requirement of predication but because of the adjectival predicate's specific need to value its ϕ-features.

Once the predicative relation is formed, morphological processes—drawing on language-particular resources—apply to determine whether and to what extent it will be translated into actual morphological agreement between the subject and the predicate. This state of affairs is captured nicely on the view that subject-predicate agreement (just like Feature Transmission under variable binding) occurs at the PF branch of the grammar, namely, in syntactic configurations that are both visible and sensitive to morphophonological processes but not to semantic interpretation.

Things are dramatically different with Feature Transmission under variable binding. The bound variable reading of (59a) is lost if the possessive pronoun is anything but [1SG], (64a). The bound variable reading of (59b) survives with a [3SG] possessive pronoun because its binder, the relative pronoun *who*, is doubly specified for 1st person and 3rd (or no) person, (64b) (see Kratzer 2009 for details). Notice that this reading is lost with a 2nd person pronoun.

(64) a. Only I did his homework.
      b. I am the only one who takes care of his / your children.

As Heim (2008) and Kratzer (2009) independently show, variable binding requires φ-agreement even in situations where the mismatch in features is semantically warranted; this is quite different from what we saw with predication. Thus, (65a) is impossible even if uttered by Nina (Kratzer's example), and (65b) is impossible even when each member of the plurality denoted by *they* is a male (Heim's example).[32]

(65) a. *Nina respects myself.   (uttered by Nina)
      b. *They$_i$ each thought he$_i$ had won.
          (cf. They$_i$ each thought they$_i$ had won)

There are two ways to think of the nature of the violations in (65). One way, common to Heim's and Kratzer's discussions, is in terms of a mismatch at PF. Pronominal variables start their lives as minimal pronouns; they only acquire their features at PF, under binding, by a process of Feature Transmission. Since Feature Transmission *copies* feature values from the binder to the bindee, a mismatch cannot arise.

An alternative approach locates the violation at LF (see von Stechow 2003, Reuland 2010). On this view, φ-features on pronominal variables are inherent, but are invisible to semantic interpretation thanks to a process of Feature Deletion that removes them at LF. This process crucially depends on φ-matching between binder and bindee. Furthermore, variable binding (of a pronoun) *cannot* occur without Feature Deletion. Thus, mismatches like those in (65) are incapable of producing well-formed binding at LF.

It is customary in the literature to take these two views as mutually exclusive competitors. However, this is not at all obvious. Suppose that the fundamental condition on bound pronouns is the following:

(66) *Semantic condition on bound pronouns*
      At the semantic interface, bound pronouns must be minimal (i.e., unvalued).

This criterion, indeed, can be accomplished *either* by Feature Transmission at PF *or* by Feature Deletion at LF. Either the bound pronoun never carries semantically interpreted features, or it does and then "gets rid" of them prior to semantics. I will propose that both operations are available, but that independent principles of a very general character guarantee that their respective jurisdictions are disjoint. In a nutshell, Feature Deletion kicks in only if Feature Transmission fails (see below). Notice that on both views, and indeed, on anyone's view, pronouns and functional categories in general must acquire a definite content prior to pronunciation. This is simply due to the fact that Spell-Out rules operate with value specifications.[33]

(67) *Morphological condition on pronouns and functional categories*
   At Spell-Out, pronouns and functional categories must be valued.

   Let us focus first on the PF route of satisfying (66), because it is this route that is used in logophoric OC and that plays a key role in explaining the OC-NC generalization. In section 3.6, we will take up the option of Feature Deletion.
   Agreement is a particularly strong form of matching—arguably, the strongest form (ignoring the trivial case of identity, where a feature matches itself). I will employ the notion "feature sharing" as developed in Head-Driven Phrase Structure Grammar and adapted in Frampton and Gutmann 2006 and Pesetsky and Torrego 2007 to capture this relation. Upon Feature Transmission, the binder and the bindee *share* the very same feature occurrences. What agreement between two feature *occurrences* achieves is elimination of one occurrence and "copying" of the other one into two *instances*. If feature occurrences are individuated by indices, the process can be represented as follows:[34]

(68) *Agreement and feature sharing*
   $F_\alpha[n] \dots F_\beta[\ ] \rightarrow F_\alpha[n] \dots F_\beta[n]$

With this notation in place, the following condition can be stated:

(69) *PF condition on bound pronouns*
   Given a PF representation containing $[_\Sigma \dots X_{i\,[\alpha]} \dots pron_{i\,[\beta]} \dots]$, where
   a. Σ is the Spell-Out domain of X and *pron*;
   b. X binds *pron*;
   c. α and β are the ϕ-sets of X and *pron*, respectively.
   Then (d) holds:
   d. $\forall F_\alpha[n], F_\beta[m], F \in \alpha \cap \beta$: m=n

In other words, features of the same type that occur both on a pronoun and on its binder must be shared. Since feature sharing may only result from some form of agreement or Feature Transmission, it follows that the bound element must initially be a minimal pronoun. (69) amounts to a well-formedness condition on the morphosyntactic content of bound pronouns. A pronoun that fails to share its features with some DP cannot be bound by this DP. Crucially, condition (69a) restricts this outcome to elements occurring in the same Spell-Out domain. Nonlocal binding is exempt from this condition and is only subject to a weaker, matching requirement (see (76)). Within a Spell-Out domain, however, a pronoun that does not share its features with a potential binder must be referential.[35]
   Although "matching" and "sharing" so far look like notational variants, they are not. Consider the one scenario where they diverge: the binder and the pronoun are generated independently with *matching* features. Feature Transmission does not apply, since the pronoun is already valued, but no mismatch

occurs either, since the binder and the bindee bear matching features. Hence, "matching" is respected, but the "sharing" condition (69d) is not: the matching features on the binder and the bindee are independently generated and so they bear distinct indices. As we will see in the next section, the interaction of logophoric control with agreement displays a specific grammatical "break-down" just under these circumstances. The fact that the matching account does not afford a natural explanation for this effect while the sharing account does, then, favors the latter as the correct underlying principle.

3.6 Deriving the OC-NC Generalization

The fundamental generalization regulating the distribution of OC complements was stated in (24) and is repeated in (70).

(70) *The OC-NC generalization*
      [+Agr] blocks logophoric control but not predicative control.

The OC-NC generalization is a *formal* constraint of the grammar; there does not seem to be any deep semantic reason why agreement on the embedded verb should block control in this selective manner. Recall from section 2.1 that predicative control is witnessed in inflected complements (71a), but logophoric control (71b) is blocked once inflection is added (71c) (data from Varlokosta 1993 and Słodowicz 2007).[36]

(71) a. *Predicative control: Greek subjunctive*
         O   Yanis   kseri   na   kolimbai   (*o   Giorgos).
         the John.NOM knows   PRT   swim.3SG   (*the George.NOM)
         'John knows how (*George) to swim.'

      b. *Logophoric control: Turkish uninflected nominalized complement*
         Ahmet$_i$ [PRO$_{i/*j}$ düş-mek]-ten   kork-uyor-du.
         Ahmet   PRO   fall.INF-ABL   fear-PROG-PST.3SG
         'Ahmet was afraid to fall.'

      c. *No control: Turkish inflected nominalized complement*
         Ahmet$_i$ [pro$_{?i/j}$ düş-me-sin]-den   kork-uyor-du.
         Ahmet   pro   fall.INF-3SG-ABL   fear-PROG-PST.3SG
         'Ahmet was afraid that he would fall.'

The formal nature of the constraint suggests that its proper explanation should be sought in the syntax underlying the two types of control. What is it about the syntax of logophoric control that "clashes" with inflection?

The analysis in the preceding section provides the necessary ingredients of the answer. Consider the abstract syntactic relations involved when φ-features are present on the embedded T head, as in (72), starting with predicative control (irrelevant details omitted; the direction of the arrows tracks the direction of valuation).

(72) *Predicative control into an inflected complement: Grammatical*

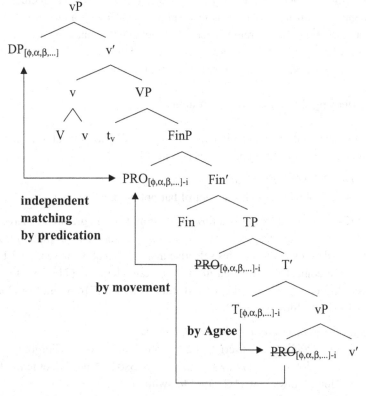

Recall that this is a hybrid representation, overlaying agreement operations, which apply at PF, on top of syntactic relations like movement and predication.

The first, bottom-most relation is established between the ɸ-bearing embedded T and the lower copy of PRO. Given that PRO is a minimal pronoun, hence unvalued, valuation proceeds from T to PRO (as in (56b)); feature sharing is guaranteed both by agreement and by movement. At this point, PRO can enter into independent agreement with the controller DP, similarly to (62), given that predication is not contingent on Feature Transmission, the conclusion stated above as (60a).

Nor is the predicative relation hindered by prior feature valuation. In the syntactic derivation, PRO is nothing but a numerical index. Hence, it forms an unsaturated λ-abstract upon movement. The ɸ-features that could potentially make PRO a referential variable (that would "close" the FinP property) are simply not part of the derivation at this stage, only appearing at PF. The structure is shipped to LF, the input to semantic interpretation, with the infinitival complement denoting an open property. Thus, predicative control is compatible with embedded inflection.

Alternatively, the embedded T is initially unvalued just like PRO is, and both inherit their φ-values from the controller, via feature sharing. This would be possible if we assume that FinP is not a Spell-Out domain because it is not a complement of a phasal head. On this derivation as well, PRO is a pure numerical index at LF; at PF it gets valued, but only after the controller has been merged. Spell-Out of the infinitive (presumably, not a phase) is triggered at the matrix vP or CP level. Since the status of FinP (as opposed to CP) as a phase is unclear, I leave both alternatives open without deciding between them.

Consider now logophoric control into an inflected complement, as schematized in (73).

(73) *Logophoric control into an inflected complement: Ungrammatical*

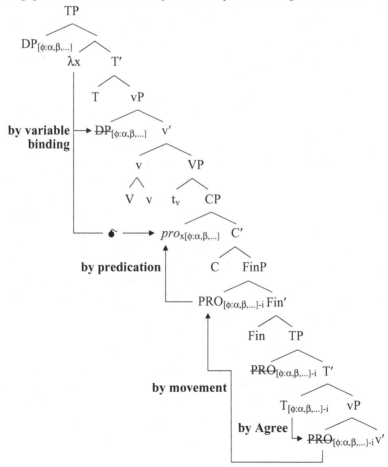

The first two steps from the bottom are as in (72): PRO is φ-valued by the embedded T. The λ-abstract, FinP, applies to the projected coordinate *pro*$_x$ in Spec,CP. Crucially, the latter is also a minimal pronoun in need of valuation. Merged with a projection that contains a potential goal, it can and must form an Agree relation with the already valued PRO. Once again, we assume that predication as such does not require feature transmission; nonetheless, in this case the process is induced by the presence of an unvalued element, *pro*$_x$. Agreement and valuation obey a cyclic logic and cannot be avoided when applicable.

The last step in (73) is variable binding between the λ-operator associated with the controller DP and *pro*$_x$. This is where the problem pops up. Local variable binding *depends* on Feature Transmission (see (60b)). But no φ-values can be transmitted to *pro*$_x$ because it has already been valued in the complement clause. Therefore, the binder (= controller) and the bindee (= *pro*$_x$) fail to share their features, violating condition (69d). Importantly, this condition is enforced because *pro*$_x$ occupies the topmost specifier of the complement clause, which is part of the matrix Spell-Out domain; this conclusion emerges independently and quite convincingly from studies of long-distance agreement (Polinsky 2003, Bobaljik and Wurmbrand 2005) and is consonant with the Phase Impenetrability Condition (Chomsky 2000).[37]

The only remaining option is for *pro*$_x$ to be a free variable, which yields no control, as in (71c). Note that this result would not be guaranteed on the matching view; on that view, variable binding would not be hindered by the presence of inherent features on the variable as long as they match those of the binder.

A question that arises at this point is why the embedded T in (73) is generated with inherent φ-features. Allowing it to be unvalued would also allow PRO and *pro*$_x$ to be unvalued at the point of variable binding, hence susceptible to Feature Transmission; feature sharing across the chain controller-*pro*$_x$-PRO-T$_{embedded}$ would produce an inflected, logophoric OC complement, contrary to fact. There is, however, a principled reason why the embedded T cannot be inserted unvalued: it would be unpronounceable. Recall that functional categories must be valued by Spell-Out (condition (67)). The embedded FinP *is* a Spell-Out domain, being the complement of a phase head, C. The φ-features on T must therefore be valued within this domain. Yet PRO is unvalued, and by the time valuation is accomplished—when the controller is merged in the matrix clause—the embedded FinP has already been shipped to Spell-Out. To be licit, the embedded T must "take care of itself" as far as φ-values are concerned.

The fundamental distributional law of OC is thus fully derived in a principled manner. It is worth stressing that the semantic and syntactic assumptions that are embodied in the TTC are motivated by evidence quite independent of the OC-NC generalization. The semantics of attitude complements, the properties of predication (more of which will be demonstrated in chapter 4), the existence of minimal pronouns and Spell-Out domains—all of these receive ample justification outside of control. Moreover, the differential interaction of feature transmission with predication and with variable binding (namely, (60)) is also an independent fact. By letting all these ingredients interact, we derive the effects of the OC-NC generalization—adding nothing more. Logophoric control is sensitive to agreement and predicative control is not, because logophoric control implicates variable binding whereas predicative control implicates predication, and variable binding is sensitive to agreement in a way that predication is not.

At this point, we can appreciate the edge that direct variable binding, the option underlying (40c), has over its alternatives (40a–b)—indexical shift and local operator binding. Focusing on the LF structures of the three analyses, consider the relation between the binder associated with the controller DP (i.e., λx) and the variable associated with PRO.

(74) *Abstract control relations*
   a. *Indexical shift (from (41))*
      λx ... AUTHOR(i')
   b. *Local operator binding (from (42))*
      λx ... λz ... z
   c. *Direct binding of a* de re *variable (from (55))*
      λx ... x

Only (74c) provides a genuine explanation for the OC-NC generalization. To the extent that theories in classes (74a) and (74b) posit explicit syntactic correlates of the semantic symbols figuring in the control relation, they may appeal to syntactic Agree as a way of ensuring agreement between AUTHOR(i)/λz and λx (less naturally in (74a), which would involve a split between the semantic 1st person feature and the morphological person features). But neither approach can prevent AUTHOR(i)/λz from being ϕ-valued internally to the complement, owing to overt agreement on the embedded T. If the controlled element is a minimal pronoun whose single morphological requirement is to be valued, nothing in the mechanisms of (74a–b) forces this valuation to be performed by λx. On the contrary, bottom-up derivations would value PRO in such cases by the embedded inflection, overgenerating inflected attitude OC complements—in violation of (70). By contrast, this scenario is blocked by the independently justified condition on bound pronouns (69)—only on the assumption that control *is* mediated by direct variable binding, as in (74c).

The point is quite general and worth stressing. The control relation according to (74a) and (the more popular) (74b) is *not registered in the syntax*, hence cannot effect agreement, let alone be vulnerable to agreement outcomes.[38] The control relation according to (74c), on the other hand, *is* registered in the syntax (variable binding must be, given its effect on agreement), hence may well be affected (or blocked) by syntactic agreement.

This is, I believe, a novel and decisive argument in favor of the present proposal, relying on direct binding of a *de re* variable (supplemented by a *de se* presupposition that C^{OC} contributes), and against the two alternatives, over and above the arguments against them in sections 3.4.2–3.4.3.

3.7 OC vs. Nonlocal Variable Binding: A Note on Feature Deletion

As noted above, the condition that bound pronouns must be unvalued at the semantic interface (see (66)) can be met either by Feature Transmission at PF or by Feature Deletion at LF. In fact, there is evidence from nonlocal variable binding, to be reviewed below, that both mechanisms are necessary. The relevance of this point to the present analysis is obvious: if Feature Deletion could apply to logophoric OC complements, it would incorrectly allow them to be inflected. The purpose of this section is thus twofold: first, to establish that Feature Deletion at LF exists alongside Feature Transmission at PF, and second, to explain why it is nonetheless inapplicable in OC environments, being restricted to long-distance dependencies.

Keeping to the notion of Spell-Out domain as a structural upper bound on the possible span of Feature Transmission, we must conclude that any variable binding dependency that crosses a Spell-Out domain is mediated by Feature Deletion at LF. Most commonly this happens with binding into finite clauses.

(75) a. Only Mary [λx thinks [$_{CP}$ that [$_{TP}$ she$_x$ is$_{[3SG.F]}$ smart]]].
b. They each [λx think [$_{CP}$ that [$_{TP}$ they$_x$ have$_{[3PL]}$ won]]].

The auxiliary in the embedded T enters an Agree relation with the subject pronoun (call it *pron*) well before it is known that this pronoun is a bound variable. The question is which of the ϕ-sets of T and *pron* can be inserted unvalued and which must be inherently valued. Since both are contained in a Spell-Out domain—the embedded TP—they cannot both be unvalued; if they were, they would run afoul of (67) at Spell-Out. Conversely, they cannot both be valued, for whatever reason it is that forces agreement in the first place. Hence, one values the other. It is actually not clear whether the choice has any empirical import; to be conservative, let us assume that *pron* is inherently valued and that T comes to share its features via Agree.

We now face the familiar problem of uninterpretable ϕ-features on bound pronouns. To illustrate, if the contextual set consists of Mary, Jim, and Bill, and both Mary and Jim entertain the thought "I am smart," (75a) is judged false on the bound variable reading.[39] However, taking into account the gender presupposition of *she* would exclude the two males from consideration, effectively translating the sentence as 'Talking about females, Mary is the only female in the set that entertains the thought "I am smart"'. This purported reading should be true. That it is not generated indicates that the presuppositions of *she* (= the semantic value of its ϕ-features) are not visible to the semantic interpretation.

Could it be that the ϕ-features on *she* are semantically inert because they are transmitted at PF? No, we have already seen that by the time the binder is introduced into the structure—actually, even earlier, when the complement CP is completed—the bound pronoun must be valued. Indeed, Feature Transmission is a PF operation, and as such is constrained by cyclic Spell-Out. This is the content of condition (69a). Because *only Mary* and *she* in (75a) fall in different Spell-Out domains, Feature Transmission is inapplicable.

This, and only this, is the scenario that calls for Feature Deletion at LF. The binder and the bindee being too far apart to "communicate" at PF, they must resort to LF communication.[40] The ϕ-features on the bound pronoun are deleted, thereby satisfying condition (66). The operation is stated in (76). Note that no locality restriction is built into it, in contrast to the Spell-Out-bound PF condition in (69a).

(76) *LF condition on bound pronouns*
Given an LF representation containing [... $X_{i\,[\alpha]}$ ... $pron_{i\,[\beta]}$ ...], where
a. X binds *pron*;
b. α and β are the ϕ-sets of X and *pron*, respectively.
Then for $\forall F \in \alpha \cap \beta$, delete F_β.

We now understand why Feature Deletion at LF cannot overgenerate inflected OC complements. Structure (73) is crucially different from structure (75) in that the bound pronoun (= the coordinate pro_x) *does* fall within the Spell-Out domain of the binder/controller. If it were valued (by PRO) internally to the complement, Feature Transmission from the binder/controller would not apply and feature sharing would be prevented, in violation of condition (69d). Notice that no look-ahead or even PF-LF contact is assumed here. In fact, strictly speaking, such a PF-failed derivation might still undergo Feature Deletion at LF, with no redeeming effect on grammaticality. It is worth noting that this derivational logic has parallel consequences elsewhere, as emphasized in Reinhart 2000, 2006 and Reuland 2010, 2011. Broadly speaking, semantic computation (specifically, λ-binding) may not "sneak in" interpretations that are blocked by the syntactic component (specifically, chain formation/Agree). The present account offers a domain-based rationale for this prohibition: within a Spell-Out domain, PF operations (like Feature Transmission) take priority over LF operations (like Feature Deletion).

The postulation of coexisting PF and LF mechanisms to license bound pronouns makes an interesting prediction. Notice that the criterion "F$\in \alpha \cap \beta$" is interpreted differently at PF and at LF. At PF, it means 'The binder and the bindee share a *morphological* feature'. At LF, it means 'The binder and the bindee share a *semantic* feature'. The implication is that Feature Transmission will generate morphological identity but Feature Deletion will reduce semantic identity. More generally, we expect locally bound pronouns to display morphological matching but nonlocally bound ones to display semantic matching. There is some suggestive evidence supporting this prediction.

The evidence comes from "mixed" (or "hybrid") nominals, whose formal and semantic features diverge. The formal features must be copied onto finite verbal agreement and, interestingly, local reflexives. Bound pronouns display either formal or semantic matching; while the choice varies considerably across constructions, dialects, and speakers, it nonetheless displays a clear tendency, in line with Corbett's (1979, 2006) Agreement Hierarchy: the further the bound pronoun is from the binder, the more likely semantic matching is.[41] Let us briefly consider two cases.

In Brazilian Portuguese (see Menuzzi 1999, cited in Reuland 2010), both the pronoun *nos* and the pronoun *a gente* designate 1st person plural (*nos* is further ambiguous between a pronoun and a reflexive), but formally *a gente* is [person:3]. Variable binding configurations may "cross" the two pronouns (77a).[42] Local anaphoric binding, however, is strictly anchored to the formal features and rejects such a mismatch (77b). Note that under a binder specified as [person:1], *nos* indeed *is* licensed as a reflexive (77c).

(77) *Brazilian Portuguese*

    a. A gente   acha   que   o   Paolo   já   viu
       we.3PL   think.3PL that the Paolo already saw
       a gente/nos   na   TV.
       us.3PL/us.1PL on   TV
       'We think that Paolo has already seen us on TV.'

    b. A gente   devia   se/*nos   preparar   para o   pior.
       we.3PL   must   REFL.3/*REFL.1PL prepare.INF for   the worst

    c. Nós deviamos nos/*se preparar para o pior.
       we.1PL must REFL.1PL/*REFL.3 prepare.INF for the worst
       'We must prepare ourselves for the worst.'

In Serbian/Croatian, the noun *devojče* 'girl' has formal neuter gender and semantic feminine gender. Under a nominative binder, a local anaphor must display formal agreement with the binder (78a) but a long-distance bound pronoun must display semantic agreement (78b) (Wechsler and Zlatić 2003:209).

(78) *Serbian/Croatian*

    a. Devojče   je   volelo   samo/?*samu

        girl.SG.NEUT   AUX.3SG   liked.SG.NEUT   own.ACC.SG.NEUT/*SG.F

        sebe.

        self.ACC

        'The girl liked herself.'

    b. Savako   devojče$_i$ misli   da

        every.NOM.SG.NEUT   girl.SG.NEUT   thinks   that

        je$_i$/*ga$_i$ Jovan voli.

        PRON.ACC.SG.F/*SG.NEUT   John likes

        'Every girl thinks that John loves her.'

Thus, there is initial plausibility to the idea that Feature Deletion at LF, a semantically based process, applies nonlocally, while Feature Transmission at PF, a morphologically based process, applies within a Spell-Out domain. This difference, in turn, explains why OC into attitude complements—a context of Feature Transmission—is vulnerable to other PF processes like inflection in the complement, but variable binding into finite complements (e.g., (75))—a context of Feature Deletion—is not.[43]

3.8 Solving the Problems with the Agree Model

The preceding sections laid out the essential ingredients of the TTC and showed how it accounts for the basic interpretive, syntactic, and distributional properties of OC complements. Chapter 4 will broaden the empirical scope of the theory by looking at the predictions it makes regarding the [±human] value of PRO, implicit control, and control shift. At this point, however, it is useful to take a step back and appreciate the advantages the TTC can claim over its ancestor, the Agree model.

In section 2.3, I listed seven major problems with the model. Briefly:

(79) *Problems with the Agree model*

    a. The stipulative nature of the [R]-assignment rule (14)

    b. The lack of triggering for the control-inducing Agree operation

    c. The evidence against semantic tense in infinitives

    d. The unique ontological status of PRO

    e. The lack of relation between OC and NOC

    f. The lack of semantic groundedness

    g. The nonapplicability to oblique control

None of these problems persists within the TTC. As to (79a), the former stipulation consisted in the association of [+T,+Agr] with [+R] and other [T]/ [Agr] combinations with [–R], (14). This enabled the Agree model to capture the OC-NC generalization. Within the TTC, however, (14) is obsolete and the generalization is derived in a principled way from independently justified properties of predication and variable binding vis-à-vis agreement. Furthermore, there is no longer direct reference to a [T] feature, its effects being reduced to the presence of a context tuple on the embedded C, which triggers logophoric control.

The triggering problem (79b) arose because the matrix functional head does not need to enter any Agree relation after having entered one with the controller, and the [–iR] feature on PRO does not, strictly speaking, call for valuation. These difficulties are removed on the assumption that PRO is a minimal pronoun. By assumption, such entities are not legitimate at the interfaces and therefore must acquire φ-values during the derivation. In predicative control, this is accomplished by predication; the formation of the predicate itself is triggered by a [uD] feature on Fin. In logophoric control, valuation is accomplished with the help of *pro$_x$*, a coordinate of the embedded context, which *must* be projected because of the [uD] feature on C and *must* be φ-valued (as a variable bound by the controller) because it too is a minimal pronoun. Notice that each step in this derivation is mandatory and motivated.

Objection (79c) to the coherence of "semantic tense" in infinitives does not apply to the TTC, since this criterion is replaced by the independent (and more fundamental) distinction between attitude and nonattitude contexts. PC predicates introduce attitudes (= quantification over contexts) and EC predicates do not. Similarly, the OC-NC generalization makes no reference to [T]—it refers only to attitude complements. There are no rigid temporal correlates of this property and so tense loses its explanatory role in the theory.

(79d) is solved since PRO is no longer unique; rather, it instantiates a generalized functional element—a minimal pronoun. Such pronouns are used in a variety of contexts outside control: bound lexical pronouns, bound reflexives, relative pronouns, *pro*-drop, and possibly resumptive pronouns and copyraising pronouns. As for why PRO must be phonetically null, I return to this question in chapter 5.

Thus far, I have said nothing about NOC, so problem (79e) of bridging the gap between OC and NOC remains. I return to it in chapter 6 but already can hint at the obvious solution. Since one subtype of OC is now understood as a logophoric phenomenon, and NOC has long been known to be a logophoric phenomenon, the distance between the two is much shorter than it seemed.

Problem (79f) reflected the lack of any explicit semantics in the Agree model and the unmotivated association of Agree itself with variable binding. The problem is even more acute if, as suggested above, Feature Transmission applies at PF and hence cannot *trigger* semantic variable binding (rather, both are interface responses to syntactic coindexing). The problem is put to rest with the explicit semantics provided in (31) and (55) for predicative and logophoric control, respectively. These meanings are compositionally derived from the associated structures (32) and (54), and are in full harmony with current semantic analyses of control and *de se* attitudes. The operation Agree, in fact, plays no constitutive role in the TTC, and correspondingly, no semantic consequences need to be attached to it.

The problem of integrating oblique controllers, (79g), was quite serious for the Agree model. It is a well-established crosslinguistic fact that oblique/PP arguments are not introduced by applicative heads and are inert for agreement relations; hence, the assumption that they control via Agree was an oddity. On the assumption that such arguments control via variable binding, the problem disappears since oblique and prepositional objects make perfect binders in other contexts of variable binding (e.g., *I talked [with every candidate$_i$] about his$_i$ prospects, We received [from every girl$_i$] the name of the boy that offended her$_i$*). Whatever technical device is needed to account for the latter cases (e.g., QR) will automatically cover oblique control as well.[44]

4 Broadening the Empirical Basis of the Two-Tiered Theory of Control

The TTC is designed to explain *both* the core properties of OC *and* those properties that distinguish its two subtypes, predicative and logophoric control. So far, I have focused on two distinguishing properties: the absence/presence of a *de se* reading and the (in)compatibility of OC with inflection in the complement. However, a theory of the sort advocated here should make a convincing case that the phenomenology of OC is truly dual in nature and hence calls for a theoretical duality as well. In this chapter, I will show that three other aspects of control—one novel, two often discussed—neatly align with the predicative/logophoric divide, for principled reasons. In chapter 5, I will briefly touch on two more distinctions sharing this profile, so that the overall empirical picture will be as shown in (80).

(80) *Summary of empirical contrasts between the two types of control*

	Predicative control	Logophoric control
Inflected complement	✓	*
[−human] PRO	✓	*
Implicit control	*	✓
Control shift	*	✓
Partial control	*	✓
Split control	*	✓

While the phenomena of implicit, shifting, and partial control have received a great deal of attention in the descriptive as well as the theoretical literature, the fact that they are *systematically aligned* with the type of control has escaped attention. These correlations cannot be accidental; insofar as they follow from the TTC, they provide strong evidence in its favor.

Section 4.1 addresses the presence or absence of an intrinsic [+human] restriction on PRO in the two types of control. Section 4.2 shows and explains why only logophoric control tolerates implicit controllers, and section 4.3 does the same for control shift (from subject to object or vice versa).

4.1 [±human] PRO

On the minimal pronoun view, PRO is not inherently specified for any semantic feature. If it appears to exhibit any such features, they must arise from the syntactic context. The most obvious source is selection: the nonfinite predicate in the complement clause may require a [+human] subject. Selection may also work indirectly to achieve this result. If the matrix predicate selects a human controller (e.g., the subject of *try*, the object of *persuade*), this semantic property will be "transmitted" to PRO since the latter is a variable whose value is provided by the denotation of the controller. These are trivial interactions that do not teach us anything about the underlying mechanisms of control—predication and logophoric anchoring.

Suppose we "turn off" the effects of selection by carefully testing predicates that do not require [+human] arguments (at least on one of their uses). Then we should be able to isolate the pure effect of the *mechanism* of control on the humanness of PRO. Indeed, the two mechanisms make sharply different predictions in this regard. In predicative control, PRO is bound by a simple λ-operator; neither the binder nor the bindee carries any inherent semantic feature. In logophoric control, PRO is bound by pro_x/pro_y, which is mapped to the AUTHOR/ADDRESSEE function; since the latter is only defined for humans, the former will be too. We thus derive the following prediction:

(81) a. Predicative control is compatible with [−human] PRO.

     b. Logophoric control is incompatible with [−human] PRO.

Evidence for (81a) was presented in (25), repeated here.

(82) a. This key$_i$ will serve/do [PRO$_i$ to open the door].

     b. The accident$_i$ is responsible [for PRO$_i$ causing the ship to sink].

     c. The apartment$_i$ failed [PRO$_i$ to meet the federal housing quality standards].

     d. The transmission problem forced the car$_i$ [PRO$_i$ to stop].

Admittedly, PRO must be [+human] under some other verbs of predicative control (e.g., *remember, condescend*), but this is an artifact of the selectional requirements of the control predicate, not to be confused with the properties of the predicative relation itself.

Harder to establish is (81b), since verbs of logophoric control nearly always select [+human] arguments, thereby masking the semantic contribution of the minimal pronoun that directly binds PRO. There are a small number of exceptions, however, and they are quite revealing.

The first example of this sort, (83a), was discovered by Williams (1992). Although Williams explicitly excluded complements from the purview of logophoric control and reserved that term for NOC into (certain) adjuncts and subject clauses, he cogently argued that whenever selection by itself fails to account for the [+human] nature of PRO, logophoric control is evidenced.[1] Interrogative complements like that in (83a) are, in fact, a species of OC and not NOC, as demonstrated in Landau 2000:39–42; hence, they fall under the mechanism of logophoric anchoring proposed in this book. (83a) should be contrasted with (83b), where PRO is licitly controlled by a [+human] controller, and with (83c), where the [−human] matrix subject successfully antecedes a lexical pronoun (not a control relation).

(83) a. *The note specified where to be filed.
      b. Melville specified where to be buried.
      c. The note$_i$ specified where it$_i$ should be filed.

All declarative verbs, I believe, show this contrast when taking interrogative nonfinite complements (e.g., *announce, declare, explain, indicate, make clear, point out, remind, reveal, say*).

Turning to noninterrogative complements, note that inanimate controllers can easily stand proxy for humans, especially when the two are related by authorship. Such examples of course do not falsify (81b).

(84) The contract guarantees to provide for all our needs.

These uses can be ruled out by choosing nonfinite predicates that can only apply to the actual inanimate entity, not to the author associated with it. Then the effect of (81b) becomes quite dramatic; see (85a). Once again, the finite complement example (85b) demonstrates that pronominal dependencies as such are not excluded in this configuration.

(85) a. *The contract guaranteed not to be violated.
      b. The contract$_i$ guaranteed that it$_i$ would not be violated.

Interestingly, the AUTHOR coordinate in the complement continues to be active even when control shifts to the matrix object (the ADDRESSEE), an observation due to Sag and Pollard (1991). While some English speakers accept (86a), none accepts (86b), even though a parallel pronominal dependency is fine (86c). This is further evidence for the claim that logophoric control is always mediated by a [+human]-implicated element in the complement clause.[2]

(86) a.   The coach promised Montana$_i$ [PRO$_i$ to be allowed to play in the
           Super Bowl].
      b.   #The fortune cookie promised Montana$_i$ [PRO$_i$ to be allowed to
           play in the Super Bowl].
      c.   The fortune cookie promised Montana$_i$ that he$_i$ would play in the
           Super Bowl.

Control shift from object to subject provides more opportunities to verify
(81b). Verbs like *propose* allow this shift quite easily (87a–b), but control
cannot shift to an inanimate subject (87c) (the intended meaning is rendered
with a pronoun in (87d)).

(87) a.   Bill/The message proposed to Mary$_i$ [PRO$_i$ to stay calm].
      b.   Bill$_i$ proposed to Mary [PRO$_i$ to join her].
      c.   *The message$_i$ proposed to Mary [PRO$_i$ to be read aloud].
      d.   The message$_i$ proposed to Mary that it$_i$ should be read aloud.

Despite occasional claims to the contrary, even *persuade* and *convince* allow
a shift to subject control (when the complement is suitably "de-agentivized").
An empirical study found that sentences like (88) are accepted by 56% of
English speakers (32% for *persuade*), and their German equivalents are
accepted by most German speakers (Panther and Köpcke 1993).

(88) Allan$_i$ convinced Harry [PRO$_i$ to be included generously in his last will].

However, no such shift is possible with an inanimate controller.

(89) a.   The will convinced us$_i$ [PRO$_i$ to respect Fred's last wish].
      b.   *The will$_i$ convinced us [PRO$_i$ to be respected].
      c.   The will$_i$ convinced us that it$_i$ should be respected.

Overall, then, the data surveyed in this section support both parts of (81),
once selectional requirements are factored out.[3] This striking contrast
between the [human] values of PRO in the two classes of OC complements has not been fully recognized before, to my knowledge, let alone
explained.[4]

4.2   Implicit Control

The idea that OC is a type of predication relation is of course not new and
goes back at least to the early 1980s.[5] For all its appeal, though, the predicational approach to OC faces a number of problems. Most noteworthy is that
the target of predication must be syntactically present but there is no similar
restriction on OC controllers in general (Landau 2010).

(90) *Condition on syntactic predication*
The argument predicated of must be syntactically represented.

(91a–b) show that an implicit object (otherwise possible) cannot saturate an adjectival secondary predicate or a derived, purpose-clause predicate. (91c) shows that the implicit Agent of a passive is similarly inaccessible to predication.

(91) a. John ate *(the meat) raw.
    b. I am now hiring *(people) [for John to work with].
    c. The room was left (*angry at the guests).

In sharp contrast, control by implicit arguments is a pervasive phenomenon (see extensive documentation and discussion in Landau 2013). In (92a–d), the parenthesized controller may remain implicit.

(92) a. George recommended [PRO jogging twice a week] (to Sue).
    b. Bill said (to us) [PRO to be quiet].
    c. It is fun (for Bill) [PRO to watch cartoons].
    d. [PRO planning the event in advance] was quite helpful (to us).

If the relation between, say, *Bill* and *to watch cartoons* in (92c) had been a predicative relation, omission of *Bill* should have been impossible. The existence of implicit OC, therefore, is a compelling reason to reject the hypothesis that OC is fully reducible to predication (see Landau 2010).

Nonetheless, a partial reduction may still be motivated. In particular, it may well be the case that a subclass of OC verbs associate with their complements via predication, and precisely for those verbs, the condition in (90) *does* hold. This is indeed the present claim. The cut between the verbs that obey (90) and those that do not is the fundamental cut between EC and PC verbs.

(93) a. The controller with EC verbs must be *explicit*.
    b. The controller with PC verbs may be *implicit*.

While implicit OC is widely recognized, to my knowledge the fact that it is limited to the PC class has gone unnoticed. Even more importantly, the very existence of this behavioral split within the class of OC verbs is a puzzle for all existing accounts of OC. But as I will now demonstrate, it is a true cross-linguistic pattern.

The case of interest is (93a). Its effects can be detected in two contexts: (attempted) control by the implicit Agent of a subject control verb and (attempted) control by the implicit object of an object control verb. Let us consider them in turn.

The very fact that OC by an implicit Agent is possible has been called into question. In the literature, the relevant constraint goes by the name *Visser's generalization*. It is stated in (94a) and illustrated in (94b).

(94) a. *Visser's generalization*
Subject control verbs do not passivize.
   b. John was persuaded/*promised to leave.

While *John* is the designated (deep) object controller of *persuade*, the designated controller of *promise* is the implicit Agent. The failure of control with the latter has thus been taken as evidence for the correctness of Visser's generalization.[6]

However, Visser's generalization as stated in (94a) is false. Direct counterevidence comes from impersonal passive variants of subject control constructions (Landau 2000, Kiss 2004, Van Urk 2013). English only has a few of them, but even they suffice to refute (94a). Note that the controller in (95) must be taken to be the (suppressed) external argument of *decide/agree/prefer*; hence, these are not NOC constructions.

(95) It was decided/agreed/preferred to raise taxes again.

In other Germanic languages, such impersonal passive constructions are much more common, and indeed can be formed with counterparts of the verb *promise*. ((96a–b) are from Růžička 1983 and Van Urk 2013, respectively.)

(96) a. *German*
Ihm war versprochen worden [PRO Hans in die
him was promised been PRO Hans into the
Auswahlmannschaft aufzunehmen].
select.team to.include
'It had been promised to him to include Hans in the select team.'
   b. *Dutch*
Er werd geweigerd om het verdachte appelsap
there was refused COMP the suspicious apple.juice
op te drinken.
up to drink
'(Lit.) There was refused to drink the suspicious apple juice.'

It seems that there is no absolute ban on accessing implicit Agents in OC.[7] Van Urk (2013) offers a weaker, more refined version of Visser's generalization.

(97) *Revised Visser's generalization*
Implicit subjects cannot control if T agrees with a referential DP.

This formulation correctly distinguishes personal passives, where the matrix T agrees with the deep object (and control fails, (94b) with *promise*) from impersonal passives, where the matrix T carries default agreement (and control succeeds, (95)–(96)). The details of how Van Urk derives (97) (from the Agree theory of control) do not concern us in the present context. What matters is the following, novel observation, which qualifies Van Urk's conclusions.

(98) EC verbs resist impersonal passives.

(98), I argue, is a direct consequence of (93a), a residue of the original Visser's generalization that is not captured by the revised Visser's generalization.

The data in the remainder of this section confirm this prediction of the predicational analysis of EC. Testing the prediction is not trivial, since passive formation in general, and impersonal passives in particular, are subject to specific restrictions that make certain forms unavailable in principle (some languages require a transitive input, unaccusative and reflexive verbs lack passives, etc.). In all of the examples below, care was taken to test only verbs that occur in the active voice with infinitival complements *and* manifest grammatical passive forms elsewhere in the language; the ungrammatical constructions are thus specifically blocked by (98).

The Hebrew examples in (99) show that subject control PC verbs form grammatical impersonal passives but subject control EC verbs do not.

(99) *Hebrew*
   a. *PC verbs*
      huxlat/tuxnan/huvtax   le'hitkadem
      was.decided/was.planned/was.promised   to.move.forward
      ba-proyekt.
      in.the-project
      'It was decided/planned/promised to move forward with the project.'
   b. *EC verbs*
      *hufsak/nusa/niškax   le'hitkadem   ba-proyekt.
      was.stopped/was.tried/was.forgotten to.move.forward in.the-project
      'It was stopped/tried/forgotten to move forward with the project.'

In German, as illustrated in (96a), PC verbs also passivize freely. EC verbs do not ((100a–b) provided by Peter Herbeck and Uli Sauerland).

(100) *EC verbs: German*
      a. ??Es wurde aufgehört Zigaretten zu rauchen.
         it   was   stopped   cigarettes to smoke
         'It was stopped to smoke cigarettes.'

b. ??Es wurde geschafft/gewagt den Gefangenen zu helfen.
   it   was managed/dared the prisoners to help
   'It was managed/dared to help the prisoners.'

Aspectual verbs in Dutch resist passivization as well (implicative verbs are hard to test for independent reasons; (101) was provided by Marcel de Dikken.)

(101) *EC verbs: Dutch*
       *Er   werd begonnen (om)   sigaretten te roken.
       there was begun   (COMP) cigarettes to smoke
       'It was begun to smoke cigarettes.'

Russian also has impersonal passives. Once again, PC verbs give rise to grammatical outcomes and EC verbs do not (judgments by Olga Kagan, pers. comm.).

(102) a. *PC verbs: Russian*
           Bylo   zaplanirovano/obeščano   obnovit'
           was.SG.NEUT   planned.SG.NEUT/promised.SG.NEUT   to.renovate
           zdanie.
           building
           'It was planned/promised to renovate the building.'
       b. *EC verbs: Russian*
           *Bylo   načato/prodolženo/zakončeno
           was.SG.NEUT   begun.SG.NEUT/continued.SG.NEUT/finished.SG.NEUT
           tratit'   den'gi na bespoleznye lekarstva.
           to.spend money   on useless   medicines
           'It was begun/continued/finished to spend money on useless medicines.'

A striking contrast between the impersonal passive of factive and implicative uses of the verb 'forget' (the former a PC verb, the latter an EC verb) further confirms (98).

(103) a. Bylo   zabyto,   čto oni   zaperli dver'.
           was.SG.NEUT   forgotten.SG.NEUT that they locked   door
           'It was forgotten that they locked the door.'
       b. *Bylo   zabyto   zaperet' dver'.
           was.SG.NEUT   forgotten.SG.NEUT to.lock   door
           'It was forgotten to lock the door.'

Let us turn now to the second domain in which the effects of (93a) are observable: object drop with object control verbs. In languages without object *pro* (a syntactically present object), "object drop" amounts to an implicit argument. According to (93), this should be possible with PC verbs but not with EC verbs. Naturally, one should test the prediction in languages in which object drop is relatively productive to begin with, independently of control. English is less than ideal in that respect, but it too manifests implicit object control in a variety of OC contexts, as shown in (92). Unfortunately, direct objects are rarely if ever omissible, which makes it impossible to attribute the ungrammaticality of *They forced to leave* specifically to the implicative type of the verb *force* (rather than to a general dislike of direct object drop).

These facts are known under the title *Bach's generalization*, which, like Visser's generalization, is false in the general case.[8] Nonetheless, (93a) suggests that there *is* a subclass of object control verbs where Bach's generalization holds true: namely, implicative ones (the other EC subclasses, modal and aspectual verbs, do not instantiate object control). To verify this, we need to look outside English.

Słodowicz (2008:130–133) observes that in Polish, controller DPs can be freely dropped—except with implicative verbs. The contribution of aspect provides a minimal pair: perfective *namówić* 'persuade' is implicative but imperfective *namawiać* is not. Only the latter accepts controller drop, which amounts to implicit control.

(104) a. *Imperfective—desiderative: Polish*

      Stąd   też   będę   gorąco   namawiał ___

      therefore also   COP.FUT.1SG   warmly   persuade.3SG.M

      do   spędzenia   tego   czasu   w gronie

      to   spend.NOML.GEN   DEM.GEN   time.GEN   in circle.LOC

      rodzinnym.

      family.LOC

      'Therefore I will be persuading to spend this time with the family.'

    b. *Perfective—implicative: Polish*

      pro namawię   ___   do   spędzenia   tego

             persuade.1PL   to   spend.NOML.GEN   DEM.GEN

      czasu   w gronie   rodzinnym.

      time.GEN   in circle.LOC   family.LOC

      'We persuaded to spend this time with the family.'

Słodowicz demonstrates that the imperfective 'persuade' does not entail that the complement action is accomplished (i.e., it is nonimplicative), whereas the perfective 'persuade' does (i.e., it is implicative). Thus, the pair in (104) nicely confirms the predictions of (93); the reason behind the ungrammaticality of

(104b) is that syntactic predicates (namely, the infinitive) require a syntactic DP to be predicated of.

One reason the so-called Bach's generalization struck many syntacticians as true was the three-way confound among "controller drop," "direct object drop," and "implicative controller drop." If I am correct, only the last of these is excluded (universally). It is an accident of English (but not of other languages) that most object controllers are direct objects; further, some of them occur in implicative constructions (e.g., *force DP to VP*) and others in nonimplicative constructions (e.g., *ask DP to VP*). Since English direct objects resist omission for independent reasons, the false conclusion was reached that object controllers in general resist omission.

The confound can be resolved in three ways: (i) show that nonimplicative indirect/oblique objects may drop (i.e., remain implicit; this was illustrated in (92)); (ii) show that nonimplicative direct objects may drop outside English (this was illustrated in (104a)); (iii) show that implicative indirect/oblique objects may not drop. This last scenario will now be illustrated with data from Hebrew.

Hebrew has nine object control verbs that take an oblique controller of the form *al*-DP ('on' DP). They divide to two subclasses as follows:

(105) *Hebrew*
    a. *Implicatives*
       hekel 'make it easy', *hikša* 'make it difficult', *hišpia* 'influence', *kafa* 'compel'
    b. *Desideratives*
       asar 'prohibit', *civa* 'order', *hetil* 'entrust', *laxac* 'pressure', *pakad* 'command'

Four out of the five desiderative verbs allow controller drop.[9] This is not surprising, given that indirect/oblique objects are freely omissible in the language and this option extends straightforwardly to control verbs.

(106) *Hebrew*
ha-menahel	civa/pakad/asar/laxac	(alay)
the-manager	ordered/commanded/prohibited/pressured	(on.me)
lešatef pe'ula	ba-misrad.	
to.cooperate	in.the-office	

    'The manager ordered/commanded/forbade/pressured (me) to cooperate in the office.'

In striking contrast, none of the implicative verbs permit controller drop, although the oblique controller is morphologically indistinguishable from the one in (106).

(107) *Hebrew*

    Gil   kafa/hikša/hekel/hišpia   *(alay)

    Gil   compelled/made.it.difficult/made.it.easy/influenced   (on.me)

    le'hitpater   etmol.

    to.quit   yesterday

    'Gil compelled/made it difficult for/made it easy for/influenced *(me) to quit yesterday.'

The obligatoriness of the controller in (107), once again, I take to be a direct consequence of the predicative nature of the infinitival complement, which in turn follows from the implicative nature of the matrix verb.

In sum, this section has marshaled evidence in support of (93a). Regardless of its grammatical function—subject, direct object, indirect or oblique object— a DP must be syntactically represented if it controls a predicative complement. Outside predicative constructions, controllers may remain implicit quite freely (up to language-particular constraints, which are crucially independent of control).

4.3 Control Shift

Past studies have amply demonstrated that control may shift from subject to object and vice versa under special conditions.[10] Favorable conditions include (i) reversal of the authority relations between the two matrix participants; (ii) a "de-agentivized" complement clause, and (iii) ideally, *be-allowed-to* complements. Different verbs allow control shift to varying degrees (e.g., *offer/propose* are quite flexible, *urge/recommend* are quite resistant). Furthermore, the precise effect of each of the three conditions is known to vary considerably across speakers and languages.

Typical subject-to-object and object-to-subject control shifts are illustrated in (108) and (109), respectively.

(108) a. Mary$_i$ was never promised [PRO$_i$ to be allowed to leave].

    b. Grandpa promised the children$_i$ [PRO$_i$ to be able to stay up for the late show].

(109) a. Jim$_i$ asked Mary [PRO$_i$ to be allowed to get himself a new dog].

    b. Susi$_i$ persuaded the teacher [PRO$_i$ to be allowed to leave early].

Despite the great variability in control shift, certain verbs consistently exclude it, for all speakers. Rooryck (2000), the first to note this fact, called them "verbs of influence." In fact, they correspond to the only ditransitive verbs that exercise predicative control: the implicative causative verbs (*force, coerce, compel, impose*).[11]

(110) ?*She$_i$ forced/compelled her parents [PRO$_i$ to be allowed to quit school].

Note that all the verbs that display control shift, as in (108)–(109), induce logophoric control, not predicative control. On the present view, the contrast is expected. Predication is a biunique relation between a DP and a Pred that enter a rigid structural relation: [DP$_i$ [*relator* Pred]] or [Pred [*relator* DP$_i$]]. No other DP$_j$ may saturate Pred in this structure. Hence the incompatibility of predicative control, an instance of this structure (see in particular (34)), and control shift. Although the testing ground for this prediction is limited (owing to the small number of ditransitive control verbs in the predicative class), it is nevertheless borne out without exception.[12]

In contrast, logophoric control may shift precisely because the *choice* of controller is not grammatically encoded in it. The projected coordinate of the embedded context is not lexically specified; only the need to project *some* coordinate is lexicalized as a selectional [uD] feature on the transitive C. The coordinate may be *pro*$_x$, bound by the matrix author, or *pro*$_y$, bound by the matrix addressee. The felicity of the result is entirely up to post-LF interpretive processes, which also explains the considerable cross-speaker variability in judgments on control shift (see Uegaki 2011 for an attempt to formalize control shift within the semantics of attitude reports).

5 Further Consequences of the Two-Tiered Theory of Control

The TTC offers new avenues of research on several topics in control theory beyond those already discussed. In this chapter, I address some of them: partial control, split control, topic control, and controlled lexical pronouns or reflexives. The discussion will be quite brief and overly simplified, merely aiming to highlight the specific form these traditional issues take in the present context.

5.1 Partial Control

In discussing the Agree model of control (chapter 2), I mentioned that one of its central concerns was the distinction between exhaustive and partial control. Briefly, EC predicates force strict coreference between the controller and PRO, whereas PC predicates allow for proper inclusion.

(111) a. *James condescended to meet thanks to our pressures.
     b. James agreed to meet thanks to our pressures.

EC predicates are precisely those that take nonattitude complements; PC predicates are those that take attitude complements (see (4)–(5)). Within the current discussion, the distinction is reduced to predicative vs. logophoric control. The task is, then, to explain (i) why PC is blocked in predicative control and (ii) why PC is allowed in logophoric control.

The answer to question (i) is straightforward. Predicative control cannot be partial because predication cannot be so. As observed in Landau 2007, this unifies the explanations for the failure of partial readings in predicative adjunct control (112a) and secondary predication (112b). Predicative *complement* control, as in (111a), is now brought under the same roof.

(112) a. *John called Mary before meeting in the restaurant.
     b. *John called Mary together/while together/as a team/extremely polarized.

The answer to question (ii) is not trivial and requires further investigation. I will mention two possibilities here. In Madigan 2008a and Landau to appear, it is proposed that PC is a type of associative plural, formed by a null associative morpheme. In the present analysis, this morpheme would map the projected coordinate in Spec, CP to a group containing it, possibly reflecting the general capacity of logophoric pronouns to enter a similar inclusion relation with their antecedents (Bianchi 2003). A semantically oriented alternative is pursued in Pearson 2013, where the notion of *extension* is applied to the embedded context tuple. A context is extended if its individual (= AUTHOR) coordinate is expanded to a set containing the original individual and if its temporal coordinate is shifted to the future or the past. In this way, both the referential and the temporal "mismatches" evinced in PC are semantically linked. Naturally, this operation may only apply in logophoric control (and not in predicative control), where a context tuple is present on the embedded C.

5.2 Split Control

Split control differs from PC in that PRO is exhaustively and jointly controlled by both matrix arguments. Furthermore, split control licenses syntactic plurality on PRO, unlike PC (see Landau 2000 for discussion).

(113) a. John$_i$ proposed to Mary$_j$ [PRO$_{i+j}$ to meet each other at 6].
       b. John$_i$ asked Mary$_j$ [whether PRO$_{i+j}$ to get themselves a new car].
       c. John$_i$ discussed with Mary$_j$ [which club PRO$_{i+j}$ to become members of].

In fact, most ditransitive control verbs allow split control under certain circumstances. However, a small class excludes it, and it is the same one that excludes control shift: ditransitive implicative verbs.

(114) *Bill$_i$ forced/compelled George$_j$ [PRO$_{i+j}$ to deal with themselves first].

Given that these control verbs induce predicative control, this fact is expected, as predication in general disallows split readings.

(115) John$_i$ met Mary$_j$ angry$_{i/j/*i+j}$ (*at each other).

Why and how split control is licensed in logophoric complements is pretty much an open question. A concrete proposal by Madigan (2008a, b) holds that a designated exhortative mood marker (lexicalized as *ca* in Korean) induces a [SUM] feature of PRO, which takes the AUTHOR and ADDRESSEE variables and returns their plural sum. This proposal can be naturally integrated with the current analysis. As long as we assume that the sum operator applies to coordinates of the embedded context, we can understand why split control is restricted to complements that introduce such contexts, namely, attitude complements. The details, of course, remain to be worked out, as well as a closer investigation of how split control depends on the lexical semantics of the matrix verb.

5.3 Topic Control

Recall that the subjecthood of PRO, in the present system, is a by-product of locality principles rather than a substantive condition on the controlled element itself (as in, e.g., the LFG or GB treatments of control). This leads one to expect that nonsubject positions will be controllable insofar as these locality principles are respected. Interestingly, a case in point might be Tagalog, which has often been described as alternating between "semantic" control (of the Actor role) or syntactic control (of the subject position); see Kroeger 1993 and Falk 2006. The former type is exemplified in (116a) and the latter in (116b). According to Kroeger (1993), control verbs that select Action complements (like 'plan') exercise Actor control: the downstairs Actor is the controllee, regardless of its grammatical function. In (116a), it is a genitive object, the subject being the Goal ('Mother'). By contrast, verbs of orientation (like 'insist') exercise subject control: the downstairs subject is the controllee, regardless of its semantic role. In (116b), it is the nominative theme of the embedded verb (ov—objective voice; av—active voice; dv—dative voice).

(116) *Tagalog*
    a. Binalak   niya-ng   [bigy-an   PRO$_{GEN}$
        PERF.plan.ov   3SG.GEN-COMP   give-dv   PRO$_{GEN}$
        ng-pera   ang-Nanay].
        GEN-money   NOM-Mother
        'He planned to give Mother (some/the) money.'
    b. Nagpilit   si-Maria-ng   [bigy-an   PRO$_{NOM}$
        PERF.insist.on.av   NOM-Maria-COMP   give-dv   PRO$_{NOM}$
        ng-pera   ni-Ben].
        GEN-money   GEN-Ben
        'Mary insisted on being given money by Ben.'

There is an alternative interpretation of the facts, however.[1] While Kroeger (1993) takes the traditional view that the voice system in Tagalog tracks grammatical functions, an alternative, increasingly popular view takes it to reflect discourse functions. In particular, the voice markers can be analyzed as verbal affixes registering which argument of the verb has been singled out as the clausal topic (the *ang*-NP; see Carrier-Duncan 1985, Richards 2000, Pearson

2005). On this analysis, (116b) instantiates standard control of the embedded subject, but (116a) appears to involve *topic control*, a prima facie oddity.

We can make sense of topic control, on the current theory, as a situation where PRO movement targets a Topic Phrase projection rather than FinP. This predicative TopP may then combine directly with the matrix verb, yielding predicative topic control, or serve as the complement of C under attitude verbs, yielding logophoric topic control. Since nonsubjects may freely be topicalized, this will give rise to control of nonsubject topics, as in (116a).

Naturally, one would like to know what makes Tagalog (and possibly other Philippine languages) special in allowing topic control; this challenge is no greater than explaining, on the traditional view of the voice system, what makes it special in allowing Actor control.[2] The important point is that the TTC affords a simple account of this unusual pattern of control, which calls for no ad hoc assumptions.

5.4 Controlled Lexical Pronouns/Reflexives

Recent work indicates that phonological nullness is not a defining feature of the controlled subject in OC, as classical work assumed. The most well-studied exceptions come from Korean (Yang 1985, Madigan 2008a, Lee 2009), Romance (Burzio 1986, Cardinaletti 1999, Mensching 2000, Belletti 2005, Barbosa 2009, Livitz 2011, Herbeck 2013), and Hungarian (Szabolcsi 2009), where the controllee is a lexical reflexive or a pronoun (see also Sundaresan 2010 on Tamil). Interestingly, in all these cases the use of an overt controllee is reportedly associated with focus.

(117) a. *Korean*

Inho$_i$-ka	Jwuhi$_j$-eykey	[PRO$_{j/*i}$ /caki$_{j/*i}$-ka	cip-ey
Inho-NOM	Jwuhi-DAT	self-NOM	home-LOC
ka-la-ko]	mal-ha-yess-la.		
go-IMP-COMP	tell-do-PST-DECL		

'Inho told Jwuhi to go home.' (i.e., that *only* Jwuhi should go home)

b. *Spanish*

Julia$_i$	prometió	[hacer	**ella**$_{i/*j}$	los	deberes].
Julia	promised	to.do	she	the	homework

'Julia promised to do the homework herself.'

c. *Hungarian*

Nem	felejtettem	el	[**én**	is	aláírni	a	levelet].
not	forgot.1SG	PFX	I	too	to.sign	the	letter.ACC

'I didn't forget to bring it about that I too sign the letter.'

Although the question is not directly addressed in these studies, it seems that this option is equally available in complements of logophoric and predicative control; note that the directive 'tell' (117a) and desiderative 'promise' (117b) belong to the former type and the implicative 'forget' (117c) to the latter. This implies that the lexicalized element is PRO rather than the projected coordinate *pro*, since only PRO is present in both constructions. Because PRO, on the present analysis, is nothing but a minimal pronoun that creates an operator-variable chain by movement, the obvious question is under what conditions such chains result in Spell-Out at PF.

A detailed investigation of the PF algorithm that negotiates syntactic chains is beyond the scope of this book (see Landau 2006a, Corver and Nunes 2007), but one can appeal to some common patterns. In contrast to minimal pronouns bound by lexical DPs/QPs, those bound by minimal operators (like PRO) are often unpronounced. Relevant cases include the operator-trace chains in *tough*-movement, parasitic gap constructions, nonfinite relative clauses, and purpose clauses. The notable exception is relative pronouns in finite complements, which are pronounced optionally or obligatorily, depending on context. A closer look reveals that pronunciation is normally forced by external factors, unrelated to the minimal pronoun per se.

(118) a. This is the man (who) I met.
　　　 b. This is the man (who) Mary thought met me.
　　　 c. This is the man who/that/*∅ met me.
　　　 d. This is the man to *(whom) I listened.

Structurally case-marked relative pronouns (accusative or nominative) are optionally silent, (118a–b). If they are forced to be pronounced, like the nominative *who* in (118c), it is for independent reasons (in this case, probably parsing-related), which are satisfied equivalently by *who* or *that*. Oblique and inherently case-marked relative pronouns are necessarily pronounced (118d), again reflecting an independent condition on the recoverability of inherent case (Pesetsky 1998).

In this context, we may think of the [+focus] feature that sanctions the lexicalization of the minimal pronoun PRO in (117) in analogy to the [+wh] feature that sanctions the lexicalization of the minimal pronoun *who* in (118a–b).[3] In both cases, pronunciation is optional, indicating that these features are somewhat less rigidly mapped to PF than, for example, [Case:Dat] or [Case:Gen].[4] Naturally, many questions remain open about the deeper rationale behind these distinctions, as well as their different expression in various languages. Still, such questions about the syntax-PF interface have a familiar flavor and are fruitfully explored in current work, a promising sign for the present approach.

6   Conclusion

The central thesis of this book is that OC into complement clauses divides into two subtypes, predicative and logophoric control. Analytically, they differ as follows:

(119) *Analytic contrasts between the two types of control*

	Predicative control	**Logophoric control**
Semantic type of complement	nonattitude: $<d,<e,<s,t>>>$	attitude: $<<e,<\kappa,e>>,<\kappa,t>>$
Head of complement	transitive $Fin_{[uD]}$	transitive $C_{[uD]}$
Control and agreement are established via:	predication	predication + variable binding

More specifically, all OC complements (disregarding restructuring) host a minimal pronoun subject (PRO), which turns the complement into a derived predicate upon movement to the FinP projection. In predicative control, this derived predicate applies directly to the controlling argument. In logophoric control, it applies to another minimal pronoun, projected by C, itself bound by the controlling argument. This "mediated route" is only available in attitude complements, whose head encodes the belief/desire contexts of evaluation from the perspective of the attitude holder. The minimal pronoun projected by this head is associated with a special *de re* presupposition that amounts to *de se*—the interpretive hallmark of logophoric control.

Theoretically, the only residue from the previous Agree model is the distinction between a "direct" and an "indirect" (C-mediated) control route. Importantly, Agree as such plays no role in establishing the semantic antecedence relation, its function being restricted to transmitting φ-values to the PRO predicate at PF. Empirically, the TTC derives the major result of the Agree model, restated as the OC-NC generalization, providing a genuine explanation for the universal absence of inflected attitude OC complements. As discussed in detail, no alternative analysis of the semantics of OC can come to terms with these agreement facts.

In addition, the TTC explains why the effects of [±human] PRO, implicit control, and control shift selectively attach to predicative or logophoric control in the way they do. Notably, the explanation rests on standard properties of predication and variable binding and calls for no ad hoc adjustments.

In the final remarks I would like to point out that the TTC offers a particularly appealing unification of complement OC with other types of control. As is well known, nonfinite clauses in subject position display NOC, and the same is generally true of adjuncts in initial position;[1] right-edge adjuncts can be marginally forced into NOC readings if set off by an intonational break. Although the relation between the controller and PRO in NOC need not be as local as in OC, a rich descriptive literature has shown that it displays the very same interpretive restriction that we have identified in one type of OC: logophoricity.[2] That NOC PRO must be [+human] was already mentioned in note 1 in chapter 4—witness the oddity of (120a–b). Notice that even a human controller must be either the author or addressee of the proposition in which the controlled clause is embedded; note the contrast in (120c–d).

(120) a.   [After PRO$_{arb}$ being spoiled in a refrigerator], there is nothing
            even a good cook can do.
       b.   The government abolished [PRO$_{arb}$ having to be surrounded by
            fences].
       c.   We indicated to Mary$_i$ that [PRO$_i$ exposing herself] really
            embarrassed John.
       d.   *The rumors about Mary$_i$ had it that [PRO$_i$ exposing herself] really
            embarrassed John.

As Williams (1992) points out, however, right-edge adjuncts are free of such restrictions and do not even require a human controller (examples from Landau 2013).

(121) a.   This book$_i$ was out of print [before PRO$_i$ becoming a bestseller last
            summer].
       b.   The crops$_i$ are harvested [only PRO$_i$ to rot in the barns].
       c.   Around here, it$_i$ always snows before [PRO$_i$ raining].

Let us assume that Williams's insight is correct: adjuncts exhibit two types of control, predicative or logophoric, depending on the configuration.

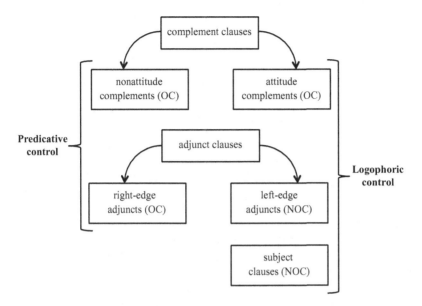

Figure 6.1
The duality of control at large

Consequently, just as complements contrast in whether or not they impose a [+human] value on PRO (see section 4.1), so do adjuncts. What emerges from these observations is that the constructional *heterogeneity* of control conceals an analytic *duality* that cuts across traditional divides (see figure 6.1). On this unifying view, NOC and (logophoric) OC are not distinguished at all at the fundamental level of mechanism, contrary to popular belief. Rather, the difference boils down to the fact that the projected coordinate of the logophoric C (in the present notation, pro_x or pro_y) is a bound variable in OC but a free variable in NOC. This may reflect a deeper, simple difference: the coordinate variable in OC necessarily picks out (via the concept generator in Spec,CP) the attitude context specified on the embedded C, but may pick out *any* attitude context (including the utterance context) in NOC. Ultimately, the contrast seems to be grounded in the fact that complements are selected whereas subjects and adjuncts are not.[3]

While much more can and should be said about the analysis of NOC, hopefully these remarks suggest some fruitful directions for future research on this and related topics. If they hold some kernel of truth, then the TTC may form the basis of a truly comprehensive theory of control.

Notes

Chapter 1

1. Another idea with a long history is that noncomplement clauses fall under a different type of control, commonly called *nonobligatory control* (NOC). These two ideas are distinct, even if their genealogies are confusingly entangled (see Landau 2000 for the relevant demarcation). Except for some comments in chapter 6, I will have nothing to say about NOC in this book.

2. For empirical problems with this distinction, see Bowers 1968, Wagner 1968, and Stockwell, Schachter, and Partee 1973:511–527.

3. See Vanden Wyngaerd 1994:246–255 for useful discussion.

4. In later work, Williams (1994) claimed that predicative control (in adjuncts) involves no PRO whereas logophoric control (in adjuncts and Super-Equi) does. He also posited PRO in complement infinitives, but took the mechanism of control there to be distinct. Although the controller is often an Experiencer and in that respect similar to logophoric controllers—"so similar that it is difficult to know whether logophoricity is relevant to complement control" (p. 95)—a reduction is not feasible, according to Williams, owing to the existence of inanimate complement controllers (e.g., *The book served to hold open the door*). I believe that Williams's dual perception of control was just right and that he simply did not recognize that complement infinitives display the very same duality that adjuncts do. His structural concerns (that a complement infinitive cannot be a predicate of the subject, being too low) are also answered within the current conception of VP structure; see section 3.3.

Chapter 2

1. See Landau 2000, 2004, 2006b, 2008. For various implementations of the model, see Adler 2006, Bondaruk 2006, Ussery 2008, Sundaresan and McFadden 2009, Sundaresan 2010, Gallego 2011, Herbeck 2011, Van Urk 2013, and Biswas 2014.

2. The discussion here follows the detailed exposition in Landau 2013:87–97.

3. Note that controlled reflexives/pronouns (Madigan 2008a, Lee 2009, Szabolcsi 2009), copy control, and backward control (Fukuda 2008, Hornstein and Polinsky

2010) are all varieties of OC, not NC, despite the presence of a lexical subject in the complement. I assume that the mechanisms regulating these options are essentially morphophonological, operating *after* the OC character of the complement has been established in the syntax; see chapter 5.

4. Note that "visible morphological agreement" must be understood somewhat abstractly, as it is not required that every single slot in the φ-paradigm be overt. In fact, it is sufficient that some slot is overt to render the entire paradigm [+Agr]. This is a standard assumption in morphosyntax, accounting for the fact that English speakers take the complement in *I've heard them sing well* to be uninflected but the complement in *I've heard that they sing well* to be inflected, despite the identical bare form of the verb *sing* in both cases.

5. These classes are largely invariant across languages, yet mismatches exist to the extent that translations of verbs do not always preserve the original conceptual structure. The lists given here are not meant to be English-specific. For example, the propositional class (5b) of English includes just two verbs (*pretend* and *claim*) but is broader in Romance and other Germanic languages.

The notion of semantic tense is closely related to (but possibly broader than) irrealis modality, which is at the core of Wurmbrand's (2014) revealing analysis of infinitival tense. I return in the next section to consider the role of tense in OC.

6. The typological study by Stiebels (2007) essentially replicates these results under a different terminology. Stiebels distinguishes between a syntactic and a lexical ingredient in complement control. The syntactic ingredient is the choice between control-inducing and control-neutral complements. The lexical ingredient is the choice between inherent-control predicates and structural-control predicates. As shown below, these contrasts translate rather smoothly into [−Agr] (control-inducing) vs. [+Agr] (control-neutral) complements, and into predicates selecting [−T] complements (control-inducing predicates) vs. predicates selecting [+T] complements (structural-control predicates). See also Słodowicz 2008.

7. Apparent counterexamples are Finnish and Brazilian Portuguese, which have been claimed to possess indicative OC complements (Rodrigues 2004, Ferreira 2009). Careful analyses, however, reveal that the complements in question differ from canonical OC complements in crucial respects (e.g., the "controller" can be two clauses up); see Modesto 2007 and Holmberg, Nayudu, and Sheehan 2009.

8. This statement should be qualified. In languages where agreement is radically absent (Japanese, Korean), mood particles play a decisive role in distinguishing NC from OC complements, as well as affecting the choice of controller in OC (Fujii 2006, Madigan 2008a,b, Lee 2009).

9. Note that neither the Agree model nor its current successor is meant to deal with OC/NC alternations in adjuncts, a territory much more liable to erratic lexical choices (e.g., in the domain of gerundive adjuncts in English, where a *with(out)*-headed adjunct accepts a lexical subject and a *while*-headed adjunct does not). More problematic are Agr-less complement clauses that manifest the alternation. Such are the complements of *want*-type verbs in certain Dravidian languages (Malayalam, Sinhala, Tamil) and a broad range—often illustrated, but rarely characterized in any precise manner—of

infinitival complements in Irish, Ancient Greek, and Latin (see Landau 2013:99–103 for a summary of data and sources, and McFadden 2014 for a recent analysis).

Within the framework to be developed below, these cases are best analyzed on a par with the familiar PRO/*for*-DP alternation in English irrealis infinitival complements, as being structurally ambiguous: the OC complement is headed by the logophoric C^{OC} discussed below, while the NC complement is headed by a complementizer that is essentially similar to the finite complementizer (obviative or not, again a point of variation across languages and verb classes).

10. The role of [uR] in distinguishing DP/*pro* from PRO in the Agree model is analogous to the role of case in GB and Minimalism. Crucially, though, the assumption in those models that PRO is caseless (or bears a special "null case") proved untenable (see Landau 2006b, Bobaljik and Landau 2009, and the references therein); hence, a different distinction must be sought.

11. I abstract away from the independent Agree relation between T and C.

12. Actually, there is one theory that offers a principled answer: the VP-complement theory of OC (Brame 1976, Bresnan 1978, Bach 1979, Chierchia 1984, Dowty 1985, Culicover and Wilkins 1986, Jacobson 1992). On this theory, controlled subjects do not exist syntactically; hence, the issue of their nullness is trivially resolved. There are, however, incontrovertible reasons to believe in the syntactic reality of PRO (see Landau 2013 for a summary of relevant arguments). Moreover, the issue is not so much the nullness of OC PRO—for there *are* overt controlled subjects; see chapter 5—but its necessarily anaphoric nature.

13. Note that this problem in the Agree model is directly inherited from its precursor, the anaphoric Agr theory proposed by Borer (1989).

14. See Landau 2003, 2007, to appear, Bobaljik and Landau 2009, Sato 2011, Ndayiragije 2012, Wood 2012.

Chapter 3

1. Bianchi (2003) observes that PC verbs are attitudinal while EC verbs are not. Pearson (2013) reasserts the distinction in these terms but places propositional complements (without aspectual markers) in the EC class.

2. Note that attitude contexts are, by definition, intensional, but nonattitude contexts are not necessarily extensional. Complements of modal predicates (e.g., (18a)) are intensional nonattitude contexts.

3. In fact, Pearson (2013) calls them "noncanonical" attitude verbs, but concedes that their semantics does "not involve quantification over world-time-individual triples" (p. 426). I therefore find the attitudinal terminology misleading and prefer to class them with nonattitude verbs.

4. The sharpness of the judgment in (20a) is potentially obscured by the interference of a metalinguistic negation reading of the second conjunct, whereby *the new boss* is heavily stressed. This reading can be blocked by using a negative polarity item in the

complement, which can only be licensed by logical negation. The contrast between the implicative (i) and the factive (ii) is unmistakable.

(i) Bill remembered to give something to Ralph, #but he didn't remember to give anything to the new boss.
(ii) Bill remembered giving something to Ralph, but he didn't remember giving anything to the new boss.

5. Some thoughts on why PC is limited to attitude complements will be offered in chapter 5.

6. I return in chapter 5 to account for the exceptional cases of controlled pronouns and reflexives.

7. To be fair, Chierchia (1990) realized that OC PRO must be locally bound (unlike other bound pronouns), a property he left underived.

8. If indices are treated as possible values of the D feature, the minimal pronoun in (28) can be represented as $[uD,u\phi]$, whose index (as well as its ϕ-values) is supplied by the controller. This partially overlaps with Holmberg's (2010) analysis of 3rd person referential *pro* in partial null subject languages as $[uD,\phi]$—that is, unvalued D but valued ϕ-features. This *pro* (in languages like Finnish, Hebrew, and Russian) must have a c-commanding antecedent (a looser dependency than OC but tighter than the familiar topic-dependency of *pro* in consistent null subject languages; see Holmberg, Nayudu, and Sheehan 2009). See also note 28.

9. This is also true of evaluative predicates, as in (29d), which, pace Stowell 1991, do not implicate the mental state of the controller but merely judge his behavior from an external point of view (see Landau 2009 for discussion). As discussed above, implicative verbs do introduce an Experiencer, but his mental state does not affect the evaluation of the complement, which is uniformly entailed. Pearson (2013:411), following Grano's (2012) analysis of *try*, encodes the intentions of the Experiencer via an ordering source.

10. Below, I consider the possibility of a third component: a predicative head, or relator, mediating between the argument and the predicate (Bowers 1993, Den Dikken 2006).

11. Percus and Sauerland (2003b) employ pronoun movement in finite clauses to achieve predicate abstraction, which derives *de se* readings on the property view of *de se* (Lewis 1979, Chierchia 1990). I will derive *de se* readings differently, using Percus and Sauerland's other device of "concept generators" (see section 3.4.4).

12. Details of implementation aside, this is essentially the explanation offered by Chierchia (1984). By contrast, Grano (2012) assumes that nonattitude complements are propositional; the reason they cannot host a lexical subject is syntactic, the matrix verb actually being a *raising* (restructuring) verb.

13. Franks and Hornstein (1992) propose that an object controller forms a small clause with the infinitive, although their empirical argument—the alleged absence of case transmission into object control infinitives in Russian—was subsequently disproved in Landau 2008. Mulder (1991) argues, very much in the spirit of the present proposal,

for a null predicative head relating the object controller and the infinitive. Differently from the present proposal, which is confined to predicative control, these analyses apply to *all* object control constructions.

14. For studies of the syntax of the left periphery related to attitude reports and logophoricity, see Koopman and Sportiche 1989, Bianchi 2003, Sigurðsson 2004, Speas 2004, Adesola 2005, Baker 2008, Giorgi 2010, Sundaresan 2012. For studies of the semantic aspects, see Chierchia 1990, Percus and Sauerland 2003a, Schlenker 2003, 2011, von Stechow 2003, Anand and Nevins 2004, Safir 2004, Anand 2006, Stephenson 2010, Maier 2011, Pearson 2013.

15. I therefore find Stephenson's (2010) argument against a context-shifting account of object control unconvincing. Stephenson points out that object control verbs like *persuade* may take an inanimate subject (Cause), in which case there is neither a speech event nor an ADDRESSEE role to bind PRO. But object experiencer verbs do not denote speech events to begin with; on their canonical use, they denote psychological events, and the controller is the experiencer, precisely because it binds the AUTHOR coordinate. Possibly, it is on their marked use, as verbs of communication, that control may shift to the subject; see (88) in chapter 4. This is not to say that the context-shifting approach to OC is without problems; see section 3.4.2 for discussion.

16. Here I differ from Bianchi (2003), who locates the logophoric center in Fin. Since predicative (nonattitude) complements also project up to FinP, I cannot follow Bianchi on this point. Notice that the ADDRESSEE coordinate is only present under verbs of communication (e.g., *want* and *think* introduce contexts without it). I also leave out the LOCATION coordinate.

17. Since Baker proposes that 1st and 2nd person pronouns are *always* locally bound by an operator, his theory is a blend of (40a) and (40b).

18. The following notation is used: c (c', etc.) is a context variable whose semantic type is κ (a tuple of coordinates). c^* designates the (matrix) utterance context, and i' designates the (embedded) speech/thought context of evaluation (sometimes called "index"). t (t', etc.) is a temporal interval variable, and w (w', etc.) is a world variable. Individual variables, x and y, are of type e, and truth values $\{0,1\}$ are of type t. Propositional variables p are of type $<κ,t>$, and property variables P are of type $<e,<s,t>>$. g is the assignment function.

19. Shifted indexicals have been documented in Slave (Rice 1989), Navajo (Speas 2000), Amharic (Schlenker 2003, Anand 2006), Zazaki (Anand and Nevins 2004, Anand 2006), Catalan Sign Language (Quer 2005), Matses (Ludwig et al. 2010), Turkish (Gültekin-Şener and Şener 2011), Nez Perce (Deal 2013), and Uyghur (Shklovsky and Sudo 2014).

20. Anand (2006:93) makes a similar point.

21. See, for example, Pearson 2013:145, where an agreement relation is superimposed on the semantic relation between the attitude verb and whichever of its arguments identifies the doxastic alternatives it quantifies over, piggybacking the feature [att]; the embedded operator then "agrees" with the attitude verb and acquires the necessary φ-features. These agreement mechanisms are not otherwise attested and are never

reflected in the morphological shape of the attitude verb. Additional stipulations would be necessary to make oblique controllers—otherwise systematically inert for agreement—visible only to this particular process. Note that I assume that agreement must be defined over *some* syntactic relation, having no direct access to semantic representations. Dropping this assumption has severe repercussions for the modular architecture of the grammar that do not seem warranted otherwise.

22. LPs have been claimed to generate obligatory *de se* readings (Schlenker 2003, 2011, Anand 2006), which would further distinguish them from OC PRO (see (25), (26c–d), (27)). Recently, however, it was discovered that LPs in Ewe can be read *de re* (Pearson 2013).

23. I am indebted to Orin Percus for stimulating discussions that sharpened my understanding of the semantic issues.

24. The categorial distinction between the two types echoes earlier proposals that control complements are not all the same size and that different types project a different amount of functional structure (Rochette 1988, Wurmbrand 2003, 2014, Grano 2012). McFadden (2014) postulates three distinct C projections; among them, his C_{Ana} (*Ana* = anaphoric) corresponds to Fin in the present system, while his C_{Con} (*Con* = context) covers all logophoric C heads, whether heading controlled or uncontrolled clauses. However, the proposal is rather sketchy and is not supplemented by any explicit semantics.

25. At the same time, the present analysis avoids the false prediction that PRO should invariantly display indexical person features, as on the indexical shift theory (see section 3.4.2). The indexical function AUTHOR (or ADDRESSEE) is not represented syntactically in structures like (54) but only participates indirectly in the semantic computation (via the *de se*/*de te* presupposition).

26. One technical question that may arise in connection with the derivation in (54) is why PRO cannot satisfy the [uD] feature on C by moving *yet one step further*, making superfluous the external Merge of the minimal pronoun pro_x. Note that this would amount to movement into a "thematic" position, Spec,CP being an argumental position selected by C. Even if such movements are allowed, the concomitant semantics would have to change, with potentially negative consequences. Thus, it is no longer clear that on such a derivation the predicate would be formed at the level of FinP and not higher up, breaking the analytic linkage to predicative control.

27. While (55k) boils down to the semantics of shifted indexicals in (41c), the two analyses crucially differ in their morphosyntax. On the indexical shift theory, PRO is *intrinsically* specified [person:1] (which is evaluated with respect to the embedded context). This syntactic feature is necessarily visible to PF, falsely predicting 1st person morphology (**John hopes to promote myself*). The "special *de re*" theory avoids this problem by taking PRO (and its proxy pro_x) to be a minimal pronoun variable, *unvalued* for [person]. This variable receives its morphological shape at PF, as detailed in section 3.5, and its semantic value (AUTHOR(i′)) at LF—two mutually inaccessible modules. Thus, no clash arises.

28. The idea that PRO and *pro* are one and the same (underspecified) element, distinguished only derivationally, goes back to Chomsky 1982; see Herbeck 2013 for a recent

adaptation in the spirit of the present study. Since *pro* in (56b) is only valued at PF, the pronominal interpretation must come from the inflectional morphology (Barbosa 1995, 2013, Alexiadou and Anagnostopoulou 1998, Ordóñez and Treviño 1999, Manzini and Savoia 2004, Platzack 2004); once again, agreement as such has no semantic outcome. Note that the arrows in (56a–b) are only used to distinguish the source and target of ϕ-values and should not be taken as claims about the (c-command) directionality of Agree, an issue that turns on additional syntactic assumptions that are not relevant here (for discussion, see Baker 2008, Wurmbrand 2012, Zeijlstra 2012, Preminger 2013).

29. Heim's (2008) and Kratzer's (2009) proposals differ in two respects: (i) For Heim, feature transmission is unbounded, whereas for Kratzer it is phase-bound. (ii) For Heim, the binder is a nominal expression, whereas for Kratzer it is a functional head. As to (i), in section 3.7 I will present evidence supporting Kratzer's locality-based account, although the details will be somewhat different. As to (ii), I follow Heim in view of the existence of oblique and PP-internal controllers, whose ϕ-features are not registered on any functional head (this was the final defect of the Agree model listed in section 2.3). More fundamentally, I depart from Kratzer's suggestion that the -abstractor that binds PRO is located in the embedded C, for reasons that will become clear in section 3.6.

30. Feature Transmission may turn out to be a special case of Agree, as Reuland (2010) argues, or not, as Kratzer (2009) does. I take no stand on this issue.

31. This seems like an overstatement. Semantic filtering cannot exclude agreement mismatches in semantically opaque features, such as formal gender, formal number, and case concord. The point remains, however, that predication as such is possible in the absence of agreement.

32. Spathas (2010) and Jacobson (2012) propose an alternative account of (59a–b), in which the apparent semantic inertness of ϕ-features on bound pronouns is limited to their *focus* value. This account does not extend to uninterpreted ϕ-features in contexts involving no focus, such as the bound pronoun/reflexive in (65a–b) or PRO in standard OC; see Landau to appear for discussion. Other semantically based alternatives include Rullmann 2008, Sauerland 2013, and Sudo 2014.

33. This requirement is consistent with the well-known observation that actual vocabulary insertion may choose underspecified or default items. The elements referred to in (67) are *not* vocabulary items but abstract nodes in the syntactic tree.

34. There is an interesting analogy between the sharing/matching distinction on the PF side and the binding/accidental-coindexing distinction on the LF side, whose consequences I cannot pursue here.

35. Strictly speaking, the claim is weaker, demanding only that features occurring both on the binder and on the bindee be initially unvalued on the latter, as per (69d). Pronouns with inherent features may still function as bound variables as long as these features are absent from their binder. Note that the "bindee" in this formulation may be a constituent of a composite form, accounting for split-bound pronouns (Rullmann 2004). Thus, in *Every one of my$_i$ ex-wives$_j$ thinks we$_{i+j}$ were a happy couple*, the bound

pronoun is a subpart of *we*, and indeed, this subpart is valued by Feature Transmission (see Heim 2008 for the explicit derivation).

36. Notice that 'know' in (71a) is not used as an attitude verb but has a sense more akin to that of a dynamic modal.

37. How can PRO be visible to pro_x if the two lie in different Spell-Out domains? The reason is that they still belong to the same phase (the complement CP). Clearly the complement of a phase head C, although a Spell-Out domain, is accessible to the phase head itself (e.g., *wh*-movement, complementizer-subject agreement). The implication is that the notions "phase" and "Spell-Out domain", although tightly connected, are not interchangeable. A Spell-Out domain becomes inaccessible to the syntactic computation only after its phase has been completed. This narrow derivational window allows the predicative relation between the complement and the specifier of C to effect feature valuation at PF, as required on the present analysis. I thank an anonymous reviewer for urging me to clarify these issues.

38. The problem is fully recognized in Schlenker 2003 and stated succinctly in Schlenker 2011:1575: "In a nutshell, the difficulty is that even though PRO is bound by an operator in the embedded clause, it still inherits its morphological features from an argument of the matrix clause. The details are somewhat stipulative on every account." This major stipulation is removed in the present analysis.

39. For simplicity, I keep to the uniform *de se* reading although the point is equally valid for the uniform *de re* reading. As to "mixed" readings, see Percus and Sauerland 2003a.

40. The implication is that semantic interpretation, unlike Spell-Out, is not cyclic. It is indeed hard to imagine how long-distance, effectively unbounded dependencies of variable binding can be interpreted in a cyclic fashion. I am also not aware of any syntactic evidence for cyclic effects in this area (unlike, say, visible cyclic effects of Ā-movement; see Boeckx 2007).

41. The reason why there is no uniform, clear-cut distinction between local and nonlocal binding is the following. While morphological features are necessarily transmitted locally, they are also visible to the matching condition holding of nonlocal binding (alongside purely semantic features); for example, discourse anaphora to inanimate objects retains their grammatical gender. As Wechsler and Zlatić (2003) note, this suggests that even semantic and discourse representations incorporate purely formal features.

42. Example (77a) does not distinguish variable binding from coreference, but Reuland's discussion makes it clear that the relevant agreement facts hold for variable binding.

43. Sensitivity to locality is found in another domain of variable binding: resumptive pronouns. According to Adger (2011), a number of languages (e.g., colloquial Skye Gaelic, São Tomense and Papiamentu creoles, Yoruba, and Edo) employ *bare resumptives*, which bear default [3SG.M] features, regardless of the ϕ-features of the Ā-binder. Interestingly, they are only used in nonisland environments; resumption across an island demands full ϕ-agreement. Adger argues plausibly that at LF, bare resumptives are

φ-less variables, which are licensed by operator binding from the local C. An alternative, PF account might take Feature Transmission to be redundant (hence, disallowed) if the language possesses pronounceable, φ-less pronominal variables. This redundancy, however, can only be detected at the point when Feature Transmission applies—that is, within a Spell-Out domain.

44. Examples like (107) in chapter 4 suggest that oblique arguments can also exercise predicative control. That predication is not limited to bare DP arguments has been shown convincingly by Maling (2001) and Marušič, Marvin, and Žaucer (2008).

Chapter 4

1. The observation that NOC PRO must be [+human] was first made by Chomsky (1981:324–327). It can be illustrated convincingly in examples such as (i)–(iii) (from Kawasaki 1993:30), where pragmatic knowledge favors a conflicting [–human] value and yet yields to the grammatical condition. Note that there is no implicit controller in these examples.

(i)   [After PRO_{arb} being spoiled in a refrigerator], there is nothing even a good cook can do.
(ii)   The government abolished [PRO_{arb} having to be surrounded by fences].
(iii) I read stories about [PRO_{arb} falling off a cliff].

2. I return to control shift in section 4.3.

3. It has been proposed that control shift targets a benefactive argument as the marked controller (Panther and Köpcke 1993, Jackendoff and Culicover 2003). This can account for (86b), (87c), and (89b), but is not sufficient to exclude (83a) and (85a), where control shift is not at stake and yet the same [+human] restriction is attested.

4. The point of this section should not be confused with Postal's (2004) observation that PRO displays "antipronominal" distribution in examples like (iii).

(i)   Microsoft went up (=Microsoft's stock price went up).
(ii) $Microsoft_i$ claimed that its_i stock price would go up.
(iii) *$Microsoft_i$ plans [PRO_i to go up].
(iv)   *$Microsoft_i$ claimed that it_i would go up.

Microsoft can be construed as an extended attitude holder, as shown in (ii), so the ungrammaticality of (iii) could be traced to logophoric control (PRO in (iii) is [–human]). This assumption, however, is superfluous in view of (iv), where a pronominal dependency is equally impossible; the latter should be compared with the grammatical examples (83c), (85b), (87d), and (89c). Thus, Postal's antipronominal condition is independent of the logophoricity condition on PRO in attitude contexts.

5. See Bach 1979, 1982, Williams 1980, 1987, 1992, 1994, Chierchia 1984, 1989, Lebeaux 1984, 1985, Dowty 1985, Culicover and Wilkins 1986, Clark 1990, Šimík 2013.

6. See Visser 1963, Chomsky 1965:229, 1977, 1980, Jenkins 1972, Anderson 1977, Bach 1979, Williams 1980, Bresnan 1982, Růžička 1983, Chierchia 1984, Koster 1984, Farkas 1988, Larson 1991, Sag and Pollard 1991, Farrell 1993.

7. It is also easy to construe an implicit Agent as the controller of an adjunct clause.

(i) The ship was sunk to collect the insurance.

(ii) Changes were made before getting proper feedback from the customers.

However, whether these examples truly fall under OC is questionable; see Landau 2013 for discussion.

8. For critiques of Bach's generalization, see Larson 1991, Sag and Pollard 1991, Williams 1991, Landau 2000, 2013, and Jackendoff and Culicover 2003.

9. The one that does not is *hetil* 'entrust', a restriction I take to be idiosyncratic. Note that while (93a) does not permit any controller drop with implicative verbs, (93b) does not guarantee that controller drop will be available for all nonimplicative verbs in all languages; rather, it states that only nonimplicative verbs may ever exhibit it. Independent constraints, mostly lexical and ill-understood, further restrict the range of object drop in any given language.

10. See Bresnan 1982, Růžička 1983, Chierchia 1984, Comrie 1984, Farkas 1988, Larson 1991, Sag and Pollard 1991, Panther and Köpcke 1993, Petter 1998, Rooryck 2000, Jackendoff and Culicover 2003, and the summary in Landau 2013.

11. Rooryck (2007) adds to this class verbs of "actual transfer" (*give, grant, confer*), but these do not easily take control complements.

12. Lexicalist accounts that rely on the notion of a benefactive role (see note 3) do not seem to offer a viable alternative. Why can the subject of *compel* not be construed as a benefactive, as opposed to the subject of *ask* or *persuade*? One can certainly benefit from compelling others into actions that fit one's needs.

Chapter 5

1. See Landau 2013:111–115 for further discussion.

2. Here is one possibility. Topicalization, like other discourse-related phenomena, must be phonologically expressed in language. For this reason, null arguments normally cannot be topicalized. Tagalog, however, is remarkable in that the topic is not only obligatory but also consistently indexed on the verb (in the form of a "voice" marker). This makes null or minimal pronouns eligible for topicalization (hence, TopP is a suitable complement to C^{OC}), the phonological requirement being satisfied by the voice morphology.

3. Many languages never lexicalize the relative operator, suggesting that the Spell-Out trigger in the English construction is [+wh] rather than [+rel]. Furthermore, nonfinite environments somehow suppress even the optional Spell-Out of structurally case-marked relative pronouns (e.g., *The man (*whom) to invite is John*); this may be another factor militating against the lexicalization of PRO, at least in standard nonfinite complements.

4. This intuition is articulated somewhat differently in other studies. Livitz (2011) argues that PRO is a pronoun (specifically, P) that is deleted by "Chain Reduction" whenever it is featurally nondistinct from its valuating probe; [+focus] makes it distinct

and hence nondeletable. Sundaresan (2010) develops a cyclic Spell-Out account of the nullness of PRO, which is keyed to the "defectiveness" of the embedding C. The function of [+focus], on that account, is to render C nondefective. In the same vein, Herbeck (2013) proposes that if the minimal pronoun in the infinitival Spec, vP is shipped to PF at the vP phase, it remains unvalued and hence unpronounced; if shipping to PF is "suspended" to the matrix vP phase, the minimal pronoun is valued and pronounced. "Suspension" is a privilege endowed by focus-related features at the embedded vP phase level.

Chapter 6

1. This is a simplified picture since not all adjuncts are alike, and certain kinds may display OC clause-initially (see Mohanan 1983, Landau 2013:226). Trivially, non-clausal adjuncts (bare adjectives or participles) do not project the functional structure needed to mediate NOC.

2. See Kuno 1975, Williams 1992, Kawasaki 1993, Lyngfelt 1999, Landau 2000, 2001, 2007, 2013, Manzini and Roussou 2000, Rooryck 2000.

3. A related observation is that a predicate may restrict the range of complementizers that head its complement but cannot do so with complementizers of subject/adjunct clauses (Bennis 2000).

References

Adesola, Oluseye. 2005. Pronouns and null operators: Ā-dependencies and relations in Yoruba. Doctoral dissertation, Rutgers University.

Adger, David. 2011. Bare resumptives. In *Resumptive pronouns at the interfaces*, ed. by Alain Rouveret, 343–366. Amsterdam: John Benjamins.

Adler, Allison N. 2006. Syntax and discourse in the acquisition of adjunct control. Doctoral dissertation, MIT.

Alexiadou, Artemis, and Elena Anagnostopoulou. 1998. Parameterizing AGR: Word order, V-movement and EPP-checking. *Natural Language and Linguistic Theory* 16, 491–539.

Anand, Pranav. 2006. De *de se*. Doctoral dissertation, MIT.

Anand, Pranav, and Andrew Nevins. 2004. Shifty operators in changing contexts. In *Proceedings of SALT 16*, ed. by Robert B. Young, 20–37. Ithaca, NY: Cornell University, CLC Publications.

Anderson, Stephen R. 1977. Comments on a paper by Wasow. In *Formal syntax*, ed. by Peter Culicover, Thomas Wasow, and Adrian Akmajian, 361–377. New York: Academic Press.

Bach, Emmon. 1979. Control in Montague Grammar. *Linguistic Inquiry* 10, 515–531.

Bach, Emmon. 1982. Purpose clauses and control. In *The nature of syntactic representation*, ed. by Pauline Jacobson and Geoffrey K. Pullum, 35–57. Dordrecht: Reidel.

Baker, Mark. 1988. *Incorporation: A theory of grammatical function changing*. Chicago: University of Chicago Press.

Baker, Mark. 2008. *The syntax of agreement and concord*. Cambridge: Cambridge University Press.

Barbosa, Pilar. 1995. Null subjects. Doctoral dissertation, MIT.

Barbosa, Pilar. 2009. A case for an agree-based theory of control. In *Proceedings of the 11th Seoul International Conference on Generative Grammar*, ed. by Sun-Woong Kim, 101–123. Seoul: Hankuk.

Barbosa, Pilar. 2013. *Pro* as a minimal pronoun: Towards a unified approach to *pro*-drop. Ms., Universidade do Minho.

Belletti, Adriana. 2005. Extended doubling and the VP periphery. *Probus* 17, 1–35.

Bennis, Hans. 2000. Adjectives and argument structure. In *Lexical specification and insertion*, ed. by Peter Coopmans, Martin Everaert, and Jane Grimshaw, 27–69. Amsterdam: John Benjamins.

Bianchi, Valentina. 2003. On finiteness as logophoric anchoring. In *Temps et point de vue / Tense and point of view*, ed. by Jacqueline Guéron and Liliane Tasmowski, 213–246. Nanterre: Université Paris X.

Biswas, Priyanka. 2014. The role of tense and agreement in the licensing of subjects: Evidence from participial clauses in Bangla. *Natural Language and Linguistic Theory* 32, 87–113.

Bobaljik, Jonathan David. 2008. Where's phi? Agreement as a postsyntactic operation. In *Phi theory: Phi-features across modules and interfaces*, ed. by Daniel Harbour, David Adger, and Susana Béjar, 295–328. Oxford: Oxford University Press.

Bobaljik, Jonathan David, and Idan Landau. 2009. Icelandic control is not A-movement: The case from Case. *Linguistic Inquiry* 40, 113–132.

Bobaljik, Jonathan David, and Susi Wurmbrand. 2005. The domain of agreement. *Natural Language and Linguistic Theory* 23, 809–865.

Boeckx, Cedric. 2007. *Understanding Minimalist syntax: Lessons from locality in long-distance dependencies*. Oxford: Wiley-Blackwell.

Boeckx, Cedric, and Norbert Hornstein. 2006. The virtues of control as movement. *Syntax* 9, 118–130.

Boeckx, Cedric, Norbert Hornstein, and Jairo Nunes. 2010. *Control as movement*. Cambridge: Cambridge University Press.

Bondaruk, Anna. 2006. The licensing of subjects and objects in Irish non-finite clauses. *Lingua* 116, 874–894.

Borer, Hagit. 1989. Anaphoric AGR. In *The null subject parameter*, ed. by Osvaldo Jaeggli and Kenneth J. Safir, 69–109. Dordrecht: Kluwer.

Bouchard, Denis. 1984. *On the content of empty categories*. Dordrecht: Foris.

Bowers, John. 1968. English complex sentence formation. *Journal of Linguistics* 4, 83–89.

Bowers, John. 1993. The syntax of predication. *Linguistic Inquiry* 24, 591–656.

Brame, Michael K. 1976. *Conjectures and refutations in syntax and semantics*. Amsterdam: North-Holland.

Bresnan, Joan. 1978. A realistic transformational grammar. In *Linguistic theory and psychological reality*, ed. by Morris Halle, Joan Bresnan, and George A. Miller, 1–60. Cambridge, MA: MIT Press.

Bresnan, Joan. 1982. Control and complementation. *Linguistic Inquiry* 13, 343–434.

Burzio, Luigi. 1986. *Italian syntax: A Government and Binding approach*. Dordrecht: Reidel.

Cardinaletti, Anna. 1999. Italian emphatic pronouns are postverbal subjects. *University of Venice Working Papers in Linguistics* 9, 59–92.

Carrier-Duncan, Jill. 1985. Linking of thematic roles in derivational word formation. *Linguistic Inquiry* 16, 1–34.

Chierchia, Gennaro. 1984. Topics in the syntax and semantics of infinitives and gerunds. Doctoral dissertation, University of Massachusetts, Amherst.

Chierchia, Gennaro. 1989. Structured meanings, thematic roles and control. In *Properties, types and meanings II*, ed. by Gennaro Chierchia, Barbara Partee, and Raymond Turner, 131–166. Dordrecht: Kluwer.

Chierchia, Gennaro. 1990. Anaphora and attitudes *de se*. In *Semantics and contextual expression*, ed. by Renate Bartsch, Johan van Benthem, and Peter van Emde Boas, 1–32. Dordrecht: Foris.

Chomsky, Noam. 1965. *Aspects of the theory of syntax*. Cambridge, MA: MIT Press.

Chomsky, Noam. 1977. *Essays on form and interpretation*. New York: North-Holland.

Chomsky, Noam. 1980. On binding. *Linguistic Inquiry* 11, 1–46.

Chomsky, Noam. 1981. *Lectures on government and binding*. Dordrecht: Foris.

Chomsky, Noam. 1982. *Some concepts and consequences of the theory of government and binding*. Cambridge, MA: MIT Press.

Chomsky, Noam. 2000. Minimalist inquiries: The framework. In *Step by step: Essays on Minimalist syntax in honor of Howard Lasnik*, ed. by Roger Martin, David Michaels, and Juan Uriagereka, 89–155. Cambridge, MA: MIT Press.

Chomsky, Noam. 2001. Derivation by phase. In *Ken Hale: A life in language*, ed. by Michael Kenstowicz, 1–52. Cambridge, MA: MIT Press.

Chomsky, Noam, and Howard Lasnik. 1977. Filters and control. *Linguistic Inquiry* 8, 425–504.

Chung, Sandra. To appear. On reaching agreement late. In *Proceedings of CLS 48*, ed. by Andrea Beltrama, Tasos Chatzikonstantinou, Jackson L. Lee, Mike Pham, and Diane Rak. Chicago: University of Chicago, Chicago Linguistic Society.

Clark, Robin. 1990. *Thematic theory in syntax and interpretation*. London: Routledge.

Clements, George N. 1975. The logophoric pronoun in Ewe: Its role in discourse. *Journal of West African Languages* 10, 141–177.

Comrie, Bernard. 1984. Subject and object control: Syntax, semantics and pragmatics. In *Proceedings of the 10th Annual Meeting of the Berkeley Linguistics Society*, ed. by Claudia Brugman et al., 450–464. Berkeley: University of California, Berkeley Linguistics Society.

Condoravdi, Cleo. 2009. Measurement and intensionality in the semantics of the progressive. Ms., Stanford University.

Corbett, Greville G. 1979. The agreement hierarchy. *Journal of Linguistics* 15, 203–224.

Corbett, Greville G. 2006. *Agreement*. Cambridge: Cambridge University Press.

Corver, Norbert, and Jairo Nunes. 2007. *The copy theory of movement*. Amsterdam: John Benjamins.

Culicover, Peter W., and Wendy Wilkins. 1986. Control, PRO, and the Projection Principle. *Language* 62, 120–153.

Culy, Christopher. 1994. Aspects of logophoric marking. *Linguistics* 32, 1055–1094.

Deal, Amy Rose. 2013. Nez Perce embedded indexicals. In *SULA 7: Proceedings of the Seventh Meeting on the Semantics of Under-Represented Languages in the Americas*, ed. by Hannah Greene, 23–40. Amherst: University of Massachusetts, Graduate Linguistic Student Association.

Dikken, Marcel den. 2006. *Relators and linkers: The syntax of predication, predicate inversion, and copulas*. Cambridge, MA: MIT Press.

Dowty, David. 1985. On recent analyses of the semantics of control. *Linguistics and Philosophy* 8, 291–331.

Falk, Yehuda. 2006. *Subjects and Universal Grammar*. Cambridge: Cambridge University Press.

Farkas, Donca F. 1988. On obligatory control. *Linguistics and Philosophy* 11, 27–58.

Farrell, Patrick. 1993. The interplay of syntax and semantics in complement control. In *Proceedings of SALT 3*, ed. by Utpal Lahiri and Adam Wyner, 57–76. Ithaca, NY: Cornell University, CLC Publications.

Ferreira, Marcelo. 2009. Null subjects and finite control in Brazilian Portuguese. In *Minimalist essays on Brazilian Portuguese syntax*, ed. by Jairo Nunes, 17–49. Amsterdam: John Benjamins.

Frampton, John, and Sam Gutmann. 2006. How sentences grow in the mind: Agreement and selection in an efficient Minimalist syntax. In *Agreement systems*, ed. by Cedric Boeckx, 121–157. Amsterdam: John Benjamins.

Franks, Steven, and Norbert Hornstein. 1992. Secondary predication in Russian and proper government of PRO. In *Control and grammar*, ed. by Richard Larson, Sabine Iatridou, Utpal Lahiri, and James Higginbotham, 1–50. Dordrecht: Kluwer.

Fujii, Tomohiro. 2006. Some theoretical issues in Japanese control. Doctoral dissertation, University of Maryland.

Fukuda, Shinichiro. 2008. Backward control. *Language and Linguistics Compass* 2, 168–195.

Gallego, Ángel J. 2011. Control through multiple Agree. *Revue Roumaine de Linguistique* 56, 313–346.

Giorgi, Alessandra. 2010. *Towards a syntax of indexicality*. Oxford: Oxford University Press.

Grano, Thomas A. 2012. Control and restructuring at the syntax-semantics interface. Doctoral dissertation, University of Chicago.

Grinder, John T. 1970. Super Equi-NP Deletion. In *Papers from the Sixth Regional Meeting of the Chicago Linguistic Society*, ed. by Mary Ann Campbell, James Lindholm, Alice Davison, William Fisher, Louanna Furbee, Julie Lovins, Edward Maxwell, John Reighard, and Stephen Straight, 297–317. Chicago: University of Chicago, Chicago Linguistic Society.

Gültekin-Şener, Nilüfer, and Serkan Şener. 2011. Null subjects and indexicality in Turkish and Uyghur. In *Proceedings of the 7th Workshop on Altaic Formal Linguistics*, ed. by Andrew Simpson, 269–283. MIT Working Papers in Linguistics 62. Cambridge, MA: MIT, MIT Working Papers in Linguistics.

Haegeman, Liliane, and Virginia Hill. 2013. The syntactization of discourse. In *Syntax and its limits*, ed. by Raffaella Folli, Christina Sevdali, and Robert Truswell, 370–390. Oxford: Oxford University Press.

Heim, Irene. 2008. Features on bound pronouns. In *Phi theory: Phi-features across modules and interfaces*, ed. by Daniel Harbour, David Adger, and Susana Béjar, 35–56. Oxford: Oxford University Press.

Heim, Irene, and Angelika Kratzer. 1998. *Semantics in generative grammar*. Oxford: Blackwell.

Hendrick, Randall. 1988. *Anaphora in Celtic and Universal Grammar*. Dordrecht: Kluwer.

Herbeck, Peter. 2011. Overt subjects in Spanish control infinitives and the theory of empty categories. *Generative Grammar in Geneva* 7, 1–22.

Herbeck, Peter. 2013. PRO=*pro*. Ms., University of Salzburg.

Hiraiwa, Ken. 2005. Dimensions of symmetry in syntax: Agreement and clausal architecture. Doctoral dissertation, MIT.

Holmberg, Anders. 2010. Null subject parameters. In *Parametric variation: Null subjects in Minimalist theory*, ed. by Theresa Biberauer, Anders Holmberg, Ian Roberts, and Michelle Sheehan, 88–124. Cambridge: Cambridge University Press.

Holmberg, Anders, Aarti Nayudu, and Michelle Sheehan. 2009. Three partial null-subject languages: A comparison of Brazilian Portuguese, Finnish and Marathi. *Studia Linguistica* 63, 59–97.

Hornstein, Norbert. 1999. Movement and control. *Linguistic Inquiry* 30, 69–96.

Hornstein, Norbert, and Maria Polinsky. 2010. Control as movement: Across languages and constructions. In *Movement theory of control*, ed. by Norbert Hornstein and Maria Polinsky, 1–41. Amsterdam: John Benjamins.

Jackendoff, Ray, and Peter W. Culicover. 2003. The semantic basis of control in English. *Language* 79, 517–556.

Jacobson, Pauline. 1992. Raising without movement. In *Control and grammar*, ed. by Richard Larson, Sabine Iatridou, Utpal Lahiri, and James Higginbotham, 149–194. Dordrecht: Kluwer.

Jacobson, Pauline. 2012. Direct compositionality and "uninterpretability": The case of (sometimes) "uninterpretable" features on pronouns. *Journal of Semantics* 29, 305–343.

Jenkins, Lyle. 1972. Modality in English syntax. Doctoral dissertation, MIT.

Kawasaki, Noriko. 1993. Control and arbitrary interpretation in English. Doctoral dissertation, University of Massachusetts.

Kiss, Tibor. 2004. On the empirical viability of the movement theory of control. Ms., Ruhr-Universität Bochum.

Koopman, Hilda, and Dominique Sportiche. 1989. Pronouns, logical variables, and logophoricity in Abe. *Linguistic Inquiry* 20, 555–589.

Koster, Jan. 1984. On binding and control. *Linguistic Inquiry* 15, 417–459.

Kratzer, Angelika. 2009. Making a pronoun: Fake indexicals as windows into the properties of pronouns. *Linguistic Inquiry* 40, 187–237.

Kroeger, Paul. 1993. *Phrase structure and grammatical relations in Tagalog*. Stanford, CA: CSLI Publications.

Kuno, Susumu. 1972. Pronominalization, reflexivization, and direct discourse. *Linguistic Inquiry* 3, 161–195.

Kuno, Susumu. 1975. Super Equi-NP Deletion is a pseudo-transformation. In *Proceedings of NELS 5*, ed. by Ellen Kaisse and Jorge Hankamer, 29–44. Amherst: University of Massachusetts, Graduate Linguistic Student Association.

Landau, Idan. 2000. *Elements of control: Structure and meaning in infinitival constructions*. Dordrecht: Kluwer.

Landau, Idan. 2001. Control and extraposition: The case of Super-Equi. *Natural Language and Linguistic Theory* 19, 109–152.

Landau, Idan. 2003. Movement out of control. *Linguistic Inquiry* 34, 471–498.

Landau, Idan. 2004. The scale of finiteness and the calculus of control. *Natural Language and Linguistic Theory* 22, 811–877.

Landau, Idan. 2006a. Chain resolution in Hebrew V(P) fronting. *Syntax* 9, 32–66.

Landau, Idan. 2006b. Severing the distribution of PRO from Case. *Syntax* 9, 153–170.

Landau, Idan. 2007. Movement-resistant aspects of control. In *New horizons in the analysis of control and raising*, ed. by William D. Davies and Stanley Dubinsky, 293–325. Dordrecht: Springer.

Landau, Idan. 2008. Two routes of control: Evidence from Case transmission in Russian. *Natural Language and Linguistic Theory* 26, 877–924.

Landau, Idan. 2009. Saturation and reification in adjectival diathesis. *Journal of Linguistics* 45, 315–361.

Landau, Idan. 2010. The explicit syntax of implicit arguments. *Linguistic Inquiry* 41, 357–388.

Landau, Idan. 2011. Predication vs. aboutness in copy raising. *Natural Language and Linguistic Theory* 29, 779–813.

Landau, Idan. 2013. *Control in generative grammar: A research companion*. Cambridge: Cambridge University Press.

Landau, Idan. To appear. Agreement at PF: An argument from partial control. *Syntax*.

Larson, Richard. 1991. *Promise* and the theory of control. *Linguistic Inquiry* 22, 103–139.

Lebeaux, David. 1984. Anaphoric binding and the definition of PRO. In *Proceedings of NELS 14*, ed. by Charles Jones and Peter Sells, 253–274. Amherst: University of Massachusetts, Graduate Linguistic Student Association.

Lebeaux, David. 1985. Locality and anaphoric binding. *The Linguistic Review* 4, 343–363.

Lee, Kum Young. 2009. Finite control in Korean. Doctoral dissertation, University of Iowa.

Lewis, David. 1979. Attitudes *de dicto* and *de se*. *The Philosophical Review* 88, 513–543.

Livitz, Inna. 2011. Incorporating PRO: A defective-goal analysis. In *NYU working papers in linguistics 3*, ed. by Neil Myler and Jim Wood, 95–119. New York: New York University, Department of Linguistics.

Ludwig, Rainer A., Robert Munro, David W. Fleck, and Uli Sauerland. 2010. Reported speech in Matses: Obligatory perspective shift with syntactic transparency. In *SULA 5: Proceedings of the Seventh Meeting on the Semantics of Under-Represented Languages in the Americas*, ed. by Suzi Lima, 33–48. Amherst: University of Massachusetts, Graduate Linguistic Student Association..

Lyngfelt, Benjamin. 1999. Optimal control: An OT perspective on the interpretation of PRO in Swedish. *Working Papers in Scandinavian Syntax* 63, 75–104.

Madigan, Sean. 2008a. Control constructions in Korean. Doctoral dissertation, University of Delaware.

Madigan, Sean. 2008b. Obligatory split control into exhortative complements in Korean. *Linguistic Inquiry* 39, 493–502.

Maier, Emar. 2011. On the roads to *de se*. In *Proceedings of SALT 21*, ed. by Neil Ashton, Anca Cherecheş, and David Lutz, 392–412. Ithaca, NY: Cornell University, CLC Publications.

Maling, Joan. 2001. Dative: The heterogeneity of the mapping among morphological case, grammatical functions and thematic roles. *Lingua* 111, 419–464.

Manzini, M. Rita, and Anna Roussou. 2000. A Minimalist theory of A-movement and control. *Lingua* 110, 409–447.

Manzini, M. Rita, and Leonardo M. Savoia. 2004. The nature of the agreement inflections of the verb. In *Romance Op. 47: Collected papers on Romance syntax*, ed. by Ana Castro, Marcelo Ferreira, Valentine Hacquard, and Andres P. Salanova, 149–178. MIT Working Papers in Linguistics 47. Cambridge, MA: MIT, MIT Working Papers in Linguistics.

Marantz, Alec. 1993. Implications of asymmetries in double object constructions. In *Theoretical aspects of Bantu grammar*, ed. by Sam A. Mchombo, 113–150. Stanford, CA: CSLI Publications.

Marušič, Frank, Tatjana Marvin, and Rok Žaucer. 2008. Depictive secondary predication with no PRO. In *Formal description of Slavic languages*, ed. by Gerhild Zybatow, Luka Szucsich, Uwe Junghanns, and Roland Meyer, 423–434. Frankfurt: Peter Lang.

McFadden, Thomas. 2005. The distribution of subjects in non-finite clauses: An account without Case. In *Proceedings of the 28th Annual Penn Linguistics Colloquium*, ed. by Sudha Arunachalam, Tatjana Scheffler, Sandhya Sundaresan, and Joshua Tauberer, 169–182. Philadelphia: University of Pennsylvania, Penn Graduate Linguistics Society.

McFadden, Thomas. 2014. On subject reference and the cartography of clause types. *Natural Language and Linguistic Theory* 32, 115–135.

Mensching, Guido. 2000. *Infinitive constructions with specified subjects: A syntactic analysis of the Romance languages.* Oxford: Oxford University Press.

Menuzzi, Sergio. 1999. *Binding theory and pronominal anaphora in Brazilian Portuguese.* The Hague: LOT International Series.

Modesto, Marcello. 2007. Null subjects in Brazilian Portuguese and Finnish: They are not derived by movement. In *New horizons in the analysis of control and raising*, ed. by William D. Davies and Stanley Dubinsky, 231–248. Dordrecht: Springer.

Mohanan, K. P. 1983. Functional and anaphoric control. *Linguistic Inquiry* 14, 641–674.

Mulder, René. 1991. An empty head for object control. In *Proceedings of NELS 21*, ed. by Tim Sherer, 293–307. Amherst: University of Massachusetts, Graduate Linguistic Student Association.

Ndayiragije, Juvénal. 2012. On raising out of control. *Linguistic Inquiry* 43, 275–299.

Ordóñez, Francisco, and Esthela Treviño. 1999. Left-dislocated subjects and the *pro*-drop parameter: A case study of Spanish. *Lingua* 107, 39–68.

Panther, Klaus-Uwe, and Klaus-Michael Köpcke. 1993. A cognitive approach to obligatory control phenomena in English and German. *Folia Linguistica* 27, 57–105.

Pearson, Hazel. 2013. The sense of self: Topics in the semantics of *de se* expressions. Doctoral dissertation, Harvard University.

Pearson, Matthew. 2005. The Malagasy subject as an Ā-element. *Natural Language and Linguistic Theory* 23, 381–457.

Percus, Orin, and Uli Sauerland. 2003a. On the LFs of attitude reports. In *Proceedings of Sinn und Bedeutung 7*, ed. by Matthias Weisberger, 228–242. Konstanz: Universität Konstanz.

Percus, Orin, and Uli Sauerland. 2003b. Pronoun movement in dream reports. In *Proceedings of NELS 33*, ed. by Makoto Kadowaki and Shigeto Kawahara, 265–284. Amherst: University of Massachusetts, Graduate Linguistic Student Association.

Pesetsky, David. 1998. Some Optimality principles of sentence pronunciation. In *Is the best good enough? Optimality and computation in syntax*, ed. by Pilar Barbosa, Danny Fox, Paul Hagstrom, Martha McGinnis, and David Pesetsky, 337–383. Cambridge, MA: MIT Press.

Pesetsky, David, and Esther Torrego. 2007. The syntax of valuation and the interpretability of features. In *Phrasal and clausal architecture: Syntactic derivation and interpretation (in honor of Joseph E. Emonds)*, ed. by Simin Karimi, Vida Samiian, and Wendy K. Wilkins, 262–294. Amsterdam: John Benjamins.

Petter, Marga. 1998. *Getting PRO under control.* The Hague: HIL, Holland Academic Graphics.

Platzack, Christer. 2004. Agreement and the Person Phrase Hypothesis. *Working Papers in Scandinavian Syntax* 73, 83–112.

Polinsky, Maria. 2003. Non-canonical agreement is canonical. *Transactions of the Philological Society* 101, 279–312.

Postal, Paul M. 1970. On coreferential complement subject deletion. *Linguistic Inquiry* 1, 439–500.

Postal, Paul M. 2004. *Skeptical linguistic essays*. Oxford: Oxford University Press.

Preminger, Omer. 2013. That's not how you agree: A reply to Zeijlstra. *The Linguistic Review* 30, 491–500.

Quer, Josep. 2005. Context shift and indexical variables in sign languages. In *Proceedings of SALT XV*, ed. by Effi Georgala and Jonathan Howell, 152–168. Ithaca, NY: Cornell University, CLC Publications.

Raposo, Eduardo. 1987. Case theory and Infl-to-Comp: The inflected infinitive in European Portuguese. *Linguistic Inquiry* 18, 85–109.

Reinhart, Tanya. 2000. Strategies of anaphora resolution. In *Interface strategies*, ed. by Hans Bennis, Martin Everaert, and Eric J. Reuland, 295–325. Amsterdam: Royal Academy of Arts and Sciences.

Reinhart, Tanya. 2002. The theta system—An overview. *Theoretical Linguistics* 28, 229–290.

Reinhart, Tanya. 2006. *Interface strategies: Optimal and costly computations*. Cambridge, MA: MIT Press.

Reuland, Eric. 2006. Logophoricity. In *The Blackwell companion to syntax*, ed. by Martin Everaert and Henk van Riemsdijk, 3:1–20. Oxford: Blackwell.

Reuland, Eric. 2010. Minimal versus not so minimal pronouns: Feature transmission, feature deletion, and the role of economy in the language system. In *The linguistics enterprise: From knowledge of language to knowledge in linguistics*, ed. by Martin Everaert, Tom Lentz, Hannah de Mulder, Øystein Nilsen, and Arjen Zondervan, 257–282. Amsterdam: John Benjamins.

Reuland, Eric. 2011. *Anaphora and language design*. Cambridge, MA: MIT Press.

Rice, Keren. 1989. *A grammar of Slave*. Berlin: Mouton de Gruyter.

Richards, Norvin. 1998. The Principle of Minimal Compliance. *Linguistic Inquiry* 29, 599–629.

Richards, Norvin. 2000. Another look at Tagalog subjects. In *Formal issues in Austronesian linguistics*, ed. by Ileana Paul, Vivianne Phillips, and Lisa Travis, 105–116. Dordrecht: Kluwer.

Rizzi, Luigi. 1997. The fine structure of the left periphery. In *Elements of grammar: Handbook in generative syntax*, ed. by Liliane Haegeman, 281–337. Dordrecht: Kluwer.

Rochette, Anne. 1988. Semantic and syntactic aspects of Romance sentential complementation. Doctoral dissertation, MIT.

Rodrigues, Cilene. 2004. Impoverished morphology and A-movement out of case domains. Doctoral dissertation, University of Maryland.

Rooryck, Johan. 2000. *Configurations of sentential complementation: Perspectives from Romance languages*. London: Routledge.

Rooryck, Johan. 2007. Control via selection. In *New horizons in the analysis of control and raising*, ed. by William D. Davies and Stanley Dubinsky, 281–292. Dordrecht: Springer.

Rosenbaum, Peter. 1967. *The grammar of English predicate complement constructions*. Cambridge, MA: MIT Press.

Rullmann, Hotze. 2004. First and second person pronouns as bound variables. *Linguistic Inquiry* 35, 159–168.

Rullmann, Hotze. 2008. Binding of person/number features. Slides for a talk given at SALT 18, University of Massachusetts, Amherst.

Růžička, Rudolph. 1983. Remarks on control. *Linguistic Inquiry* 14, 309–324.

Safir, Ken. 2004. Person, context and perspective. *Rivista di Linguistica* 16, 107–153.

Safir, Ken. 2010. PRO and *de se*. Ms., Rutgers University.

Sag, Ivan, and Carl Pollard. 1991. An integrated theory of complement control. *Language* 67, 63–113.

Sato, Yosuke. 2011. On the movement theory of control: Voices from Standard Indonesian. *Canadian Journal of Linguistics* 56, 267–275.

Sauerland, Uli. 2013. Presuppositions and the alternative tier. In *Proceedings of SALT 23*, ed. by Anca Chereches, Neil Ashton, and David Lutz, 156–173. Ithaca, NY: Cornell University, CLC Publications.

Schlenker, Philippe. 2003. A plea for monsters. *Linguistics and Philosophy* 26, 29–120.

Schlenker, Philippe. 2011. Indexicality and *de se* reports. In *Semantics: An international handbook of natural language meaning*, ed. by Klaus von Heusinger, Claudia Maienborn, and Paul Portner, 1561–1604. Berlin: Mouton de Gruyter.

Sells, Peter. 1987. Aspects of logophoricity. *Linguistic Inquiry* 18, 445–480.

Shklovsky, Kirill, and Yasutada Sudo. 2014. The syntax of monsters. *Linguistic Inquiry* 45, 381–402.

Sigurðsson, Halldór Ármann. 2004. The syntax of person, tense and speech features. *Rivista di Linguistica* 16, 219–251.

Sigurðsson, Halldór Ármann. 2006. Agree in syntax, agreement in signs. In *Agreement systems*, ed. by Cedric Boeckx, 201–237. Amsterdam: John Benjamins.

Sigurðsson, Halldór Ármann. 2008. The Case of PRO. *Natural Language and Linguistic Theory* 26, 403–450.

Sigurðsson, Halldór Ármann. 2009. Remarks on features. In *Explorations of phase theory: Features and arguments*, ed. by Kleanthes K. Grohmann, 21–52. Berlin: Mouton de Gruyter.

Sigurðsson, Halldór Ármann. 2011. Conditions on argument drop. *Linguistic Inquiry* 42, 267–304.

Šimík, Radek. 2013. The PRO-*wh* connection in modal existential *wh*-constructions. *Natural Language and Linguistic Theory* 31, 1163–1205.

Słodowicz, Szymon. 2007. Complement control in Turkish. In *Studies in complement control*, ed. by Barbara Stiebels, 125–157. ZAS Papers in Linguistics 47. Berlin: ZAS (Zentrum für allgemeine Wissenschaft).

Słodowicz, Szymon. 2008. *Control in Polish complement clauses*. Munich: Verlag Otto Sagner.

Spathas, Georgios. 2010. *Focus on anaphora*. Utrecht: LOT.

Speas, Margaret. 2000. Person and point of view in Navajo verbs. In *Papers in honor of Ken Hale*, ed. by Andrew Carnie, Eloise Jelinek, and Mary Willie, 19–38. MIT Working Papers on Endangered and Less Familiar Languages 1. Cambridge, MA: MIT, MIT Working Papers in Linguistics.

Speas, Margaret. 2004. Evidentiality, logophoricity and syntactic representation of pragmatic features. *Lingua* 114, 255–276.

Stephenson, Tamina. 2010. Control in centred worlds. *Journal of Semantics* 27, 409–436.

Stiebels, Barbara. 2007. Towards a typology of complement control. In *Studies in complement control*, ed. by Barbara Stiebels, 1–80. ZAS Papers in Linguistics 47. Berlin: ZAS (Zentrum für allgemeine Wissenschaft).

Stockwell, Robert P., Paul Schachter, and Barbara Hall Partee. 1973. *The major syntactic structures of English*. New York: Holt, Rinehart and Winston.

Stowell, Tim. 1982. The tense of infinitives. *Linguistic Inquiry* 13, 561–570.

Stowell, Tim. 1991. The alignment of arguments in Adjective Phrases. In *Perspectives on phrase structure: Heads and licensing*, ed. by Susan Rothstein, 105–135. San Diego, CA: Academic Press.

Sudo, Yasutada. 2014. Dependent plural pronouns with Skolemized choice functions. *Natural Language Semantics* 22, 265–297.

Sundaresan, Sandhya. 2010. A phase-based account of the PRO/anaphor distinction. In *Proceedings of ConSOLE XVIII*, 1–19. Student Organization of Linguistics in Europe, University of Leiden.

Sundaresan, Sandhya. 2012. Context and (co)reference in the syntax and its interfaces. Doctoral dissertation, University of Stuttgart and University of Tromsø.

Sundaresan, Sandhya, and Thomas McFadden. 2009. Subject distribution in Tamil and other languages: Selection vs. Case. *Journal of South Asian Linguistics* 2, 5–34.

Szabolcsi, Anna. 2009. Overt nominative subjects in infinitival complements: Data, diagnostics, and preliminary analyses. In *Papers in syntax*, ed. by Patricia Irwin and Violeta Vasquéz Rojas Maldonado, 1–55. NYU Working Papers in Linguistics 2. New York: New York University, Department of Linguistics.

Tallerman, Maggie. 1998. The uniform case-licensing of subjects in Welsh. *The Linguistic Review* 15, 69–133.

Tóth, Ildikó. 2000. Inflected infinitives in Hungarian. Doctoral dissertation, TILDIL, Tilburg University.

Uegaki, Wataru. 2011. Controller shift in centered-world semantics. Ms., MIT.

Uriagereka, Juan. 1995. An F position in Western Romance. In *Discourse configurational languages*, ed. by Katalin É. Kiss, 153–175. Oxford: Oxford University Press.

Urk, Coppe van. 2013. Visser's generalization: The syntax of control and the passive. *Linguistic Inquiry* 44, 168–178.

Ussery, Cherlon. 2008. What it means to agree: The behavior of case and phi features in Icelandic control. In *Proceedings of WCCFL 26*, ed. by Charles B. Chang and Hannah J. Haynie, 480–488. Somerville, MA: Cascadilla Press.

Vanden Wyngaerd, Guido J. 1994. *PRO-legomena*. Berlin: Mouton de Gruyter.

Varlokosta, Spyridoula. 1993. Control in Modern Greek. In *University of Maryland working papers in linguistics 1*, ed. by Carol A. Mason, Susan M. Powers, and Cristina Schmitt, 144–163. College Park: University of Maryland, Department of Linguistics.

Visser, Fredericus T. 1963. *An historical syntax of the English language*. Leiden: E. J. Brill.

von Stechow, Arnim. 2003. Feature deletion under semantic binding. In *Proceedings of NELS 33*, ed. by Makoto Kadowaki and Shigeto Kawahara, 377–403. Amherst: University of Massachusetts, Graduate Linguistic Student Association.

Wagner, K. Heinz. 1968. Verb Phrase complementation: A criticism. *Journal of Linguistics* 4, 88–92.

Wechsler, Stephen, and Larisa Zlatić. 2003. *The many faces of agreement*. Stanford, CA: CSLI Publications.

Williams, Edwin. 1980. Predication. *Linguistic Inquiry* 11, 203–238.

Williams, Edwin. 1987. Implicit arguments, the binding theory and control. *Natural Language and Linguistic Theory* 5, 151–180.

Williams, Edwin. 1991. The argument-bound empty categories. In *Principles and parameters in comparative grammar*, ed. by Robert Freidin, 77–98. Cambridge, MA: MIT Press.

Williams, Edwin. 1992. Adjunct control. In *Control and grammar*, ed. by Richard Larson, Sabine Iatridou, Utpal Lahiri, and James Higginbotham, 297–322. Dordrecht: Kluwer.

Williams, Edwin. 1994. *Thematic structure in syntax*. Cambridge, MA: MIT Press.

Wood, Jim. 2012. Against the movement theory of control: Another argument from Icelandic. *Linguistic Inquiry* 43, 322–330.

Wurmbrand, Susi. 2003. *Infinitives: Restructuring and clause structure*. New York: Mouton de Gruyter.

Wurmbrand, Susi. 2012. Agree(ment): Looking up or looking down? Ms., University of Connecticut.

Wurmbrand, Susi. 2014. Tense and aspect in English infinitives. *Linguistic Inquiry* 45, 403–447.

Yang, Dong-Whee. 1985. On the integrity of control theory. In *Proceedings of NELS 15*, ed. by Stephen Berman, Jae-Woong Choe, and Joyce McDonough, 389–408. Amherst: University of Massachusetts, Graduate Linguistic Student Association.

Zeijlstra, Hedde. 2012. There is only one way to agree. *The Linguistic Review* 29, 491–539.

Linguistic Inquiry Monographs

Samuel Jay Keyser, general editor

Index

Printed in the United States
by Baker & Taylor Publisher Services